MEETING JESUS THROUGH THE JESSE TREE

Stories and activities for Advent

ANNE E. NEUBERGER

NEW LONDON, CT 06320
WWW.23RDPUBLICATIONS.COM

Dedication

To Leo, Janet, Tobias and Joyana Jacoby, family ritualists extraordinaire! And now to those they are encircling into their family.

Acknowledgments

The author would like to thank those who shared their experiences with the first edition of this book: Jill Konicke-Butkus, Mary Ann Keiser, Kris Berggren, Linda Knowles-Mayers, Joyana Jacoby Dvorak, and Janet Jacoby.

Special thanks to her daughter Lucia, whose creativity helped shape the tree variations and whose enthusiasm for the ancient stories helped bring them to these pages.

TWENTY-THIRD PUBLICATIONS
A Division of Bayard
One Montauk Avenue, Suite 200
New London, CT 06320
(860) 437-3012 or (800) 321-0411
www.23rdpublications.com

Copyright ©2013 Anne E. Neuberger. All rights reserved.
No part of this publication may be reproduced in any manner without prior written permission of the publisher.
Write to the Permissions Editor.

ISBN: 978-1-58595-917-4
Library of Congress Control Number: 2013941704
Printed in the U.S.A.

CONTENTS

Introduction 4

Using the Jesse Tree 5
- *Families at Home*
- *Religious Education Classes*
- *Catholic Schools*
- *Family Advent Workshops*

Methods and Materials 7
- *Drawing Your Tree*
- *An Advent Calendar*
- *Using a Time Line*
- *Three-Dimensional Decorations*
- *Medallion Tree*
- *Felt Banners*
- *A Jesse Tree Booklet*

The Stories
- CREATION 12
- ADAM AND EVE 14
- NOAH 17
- ABRAHAM 21
- SARAH 23
- JACOB 25
- RACHEL AND LEAH 27
- JOSEPH 30
- MOSES 33
- RUTH 37
- SAMUEL 40
- DAVID 42
- SOLOMON 46
- ELIJAH 49
- ISAIAH 52
- NEHEMIAH 54
- JONAH 58
- ESTHER 62
- TOBIAS 65
- DANIEL 68
- ZECHARIAH AND ELIZABETH 71
- MARY 74
- JOSEPH 76
- JESUS 79

Additional Suggestions 83
- *Symbol Ideas*

The Jesse Tree

Advent — **THE LONG NIGHT WATCH, THE WAITING TIME, THE YEARNING FOR THE COMING OF CHRISTMAS AND FOR THE SECOND COMING OF CHRIST.**

Each year we are challenged to experience this waiting time despite a pervasive atmosphere of instant gratification called "the holiday season." In a secular society children may be lacking knowledge of their roots and may not be aware of the value of religious rituals and traditions. This is perhaps most obvious in the weeks before Christmas when the church calls for waiting, longing, and expectation. Where does one start to give Christian children these precious experiences? The ancient communities of Israel handed down their beliefs in the same way that Jesus himself taught: through story.

The Advent custom called the "Jesse Tree" uses stories to help children develop a stronger sense of who Jesus is and who were the people on the path before him. Named for King David's father, the Jesse Tree is a representation of Christ's family tree, suggested by the prophet's words, "There shall come forth a shoot from the root of Jesse" (Isaiah 11:1).

These stories become a way for children to experience God's presence themselves. As the tales unfold—as Noah's difficulties, Leah's concerns, Jonah's frustrations, and Esther's fears become real to listeners—God's plan in all people's lives becomes clearer. Child listeners can begin to feel this in their own lives.

The Jesse Tree also gives children a sense of salvation history, of the centuries before the birth of Christ, of God's plan and preparation in human history for the birth of Christ. All history is important, for it tells us what has happened, what to avoid, and why we are who we are. Stories from our religious history provide us with a framework for our belief system. These tales, handed down from generation to generation, give us the accumulated wisdom of centuries of living.

While they listen to the stories, our children are in the company of people who sought answers to hard questions and strove to be faithful no matter the difficulties. In telling our children these stories, we give them their place among the people of God.

Using the Jesse Tree

The essential elements of the Jesse Tree are stories and symbols of those stories. Creating the tree and symbols can be as simple or as elaborate as time and ages of children allow. There are numerous ways to do this; the tradition lends itself to a variety of settings. Choose the method that works best for you, or use this book as a springboard for your own ideas.

Most importantly, remember the significance of the ancient stories. You are passing on something very precious, making possible a link between the past and the future. Read each story to yourself first, becoming familiar with it so you can then read it aloud, presenting the characters so that they come alive through your expression. Tell the stories with reverence, drama, humor, and love.

FAMILIES AT HOME

Jesse Tree stories can be bedtime or dinnertime reading during Advent. For families with younger children, a shorter version is offered for some of the longer stories.

Working with varying ages in a family calls for flexibility. Some older children may be reluctant to participate in the artistic aspects. Read the stories when the whole family is together already. You are then still passing on the stories. If they choose not to make symbols, ask them to set up the tree or to assist a younger child. Preschoolers will likely join in with enthusiasm. Their efforts may not yield recognizable symbols, but the groundwork has been laid for an appreciation of the biblical stories. Offer them the same materials as older children and enjoy their creations; give them the honor of hanging them on the tree.

Suggestions:
- See "Methods and Materials" on page 7.
- Read the story aloud, and then spend time with your children creating the symbols; or a family member can pre-make symbols that can be used from year to year. The symbol for the evening's story can then be ceremoniously placed on the tree. Either way, a sense of anticipation and of a connection to Jesus is clear.
- Some families wait until Christmas Eve to put up their Christmas tree, as it is a symbol of Christ. During Advent, the Jesse tree can stand where the Christmas tree will eventually be, emphasizing that it is a symbol of those who went before Christ, waiting.
- Families who put up their Christmas tree early in Advent could choose to decorate it at first only with the Jesse Tree symbols. Christmas decorations could then be added just before Christmas Eve. Again, this would emphasize that Advent is a time of preparing for Jesus, just as Abraham, David, Ruth, etc., were preparing for the Messiah.

RELIGIOUS EDUCATION CLASSES

Suggestions:
- Given that classes meet four times in Advent, four to eight stories and symbols could be used. Whichever stories you choose, tell them in

chronological order. Decide on a method that best suits the time constraints and abilities of the children. See "Methods and Materials" on page 7.
- Send home with children a list of the Scripture verses for stories that cannot be read in class. Encourage children and parents to read them together.
- For some classes, the Jesse Tree can become the curriculum focus for Advent, leaving ample opportunity for art and story. For situations where time is more limited, a time line or an Advent calendar form will be helpful (again, see "Methods and Materials").

CATHOLIC SCHOOLS

In this setting, the Jesse Tree stories can become a central part of daily Advent observances. It will be easier to use all the stories and to create all the symbols, since children gather daily. In classes where the curriculum explores the Old Testament, the Jesse Tree stories will certainly enhance this study.

Suggestions:

- For situations where teachers want to read the stories but cannot spend additional class time on making symbols, the time line or Advent calendar can work well. One child could be chosen each day to add to the time line or open the calendar door.
- Creating more involved symbols can still be done in classrooms where time is a factor. Use art classes prior to Advent to make symbols. Methods for doing it this way would be felt banners, three-dimensional decorations, or a medallion tree.

FAMILY ADVENT WORKSHOPS

Jesse Tree stories can be part of a memorable Advent afternoon for families. It offers an opportunity of community sharing of the ancient tales and calming, creative time.

Organizers will need to decide how to stage this event based on the size of their parishes, age groupings, etc. For large parishes, it might work best for families to produce individual trees and symbols to take home, thus starting a tradition for Advents to come. In smaller parishes this can also be done, or have the group work together to produce symbols to display on a parish Jesse Tree. Each Sunday in Advent, families take turns hanging their symbols on the parish tree during Mass.

Suggestions:

- The workshop leader chooses which stories to use (there will not be time for all twenty-four stories) and prepares one or more people to be storytellers.
- If the group is large, choose two or three methods for making Jesse Trees and set up stations for each, providing the materials needed.
- Open and close with prayer. Look into Advent blessing prayers or use Advent Scriptures.
- If possible, provide music to sing during prayer time, and soft music while people are working on the symbols.
- Depending on the length of this workshop, also provide healthy snacks.

Methods and Materials

The Jesse Tree does not require expensive or elaborate materials. It can be a process that is as simple or as involved as the participants choose. The following are several methods for making the tree and symbols. Select one or use the ideas as a springboard for your own plan. Most importantly, enjoy the stories and the creativity!

Drawing your tree

AGE LEVEL FOR CREATING THIS
Ages 3 to adult

TYPES OF GROUPS
- those with various ages
- preschool and elementary classes
- families
- parish workshops

MATERIALS
For the drawings:
- paper
- pencils, markers or crayons
- or symbols (see pages 84-95)
- thread or ribbon
- tape or magnets

For the tree (choose one):
- deciduous tree branch secured in a bucket of wet sand, onto a bulletin board, etc.
- Christmas tree
- green poster board cut into the shape of an evergreen

DIRECTIONS AND DISPLAY
Read the story with the children; then have them draw or color. This tends to be the most calming of the projects.

You can display the drawings in a number of ways:
- To hang onto a branch or actual tree, tape ribbon or thread to form a loop on the drawing
- For a poster board tree, simply tape the symbols on; if the tree is adhered to a metal surface, use magnets

One of the charms of having children draw ideas from the story is that they bring their own interpretations, such as war planes flying over David and Goliath or spectacles on Abraham. With very young children, ask them to interpret their drawings for you, and write their words on the back of the drawings. These drawings can be saved and will be a treasure in years to come.

An Advent Calendar

Advent calendars have little "doors" to be opened each day in Advent; adapt this concept for a Jesse Tree.

AGE LEVEL FOR CREATING THIS
Ages 6 and up

TYPES OF GROUPS
- families who don't have time for a daily art project
- religion classes where time is restricted

MATERIALS

- one sheet of white or light-colored poster board (28" x 22")
- a pencil
- markers of various bright colors (including green)
- twenty-four three-inch square sheets of paper and tape (or Post-It Notes)
- symbols (see pages 84-95)
- tacks for hanging the poster

DIRECTIONS AND DISPLAY

With a pencil, draw a simple outline of an evergreen tree onto the poster board. Outline it with a green marker.

With bright markers, draw symbols for each story directly onto the poster. These must be less than 3 inches square, or use the provided symbols. Start with a Creation symbol on the base of the tree, and Christ's symbol at the very top. Use the Table of Contents to follow the order of the stories, so Adam and Eve and Noah symbols are at the bottom of the tree near the Creation symbols and Joseph and Mary symbols are near the top where the Jesus symbol is.

Onto the 3-inch papers, write the numbers 1, or 2, etc., up to number 24, or the names of each story character. Place these "doors" over the symbols, corresponding the number or name on the door to the symbol.

Hang the poster and, after reading a story, have children guess the symbol and take off the little door. Little by little, the tree will be seen as decorated with colorful symbols. The poster can be saved from year to year.

Using a time line

AGE LEVEL FOR CREATING THIS
Ages 9 to adult

TYPES OF GROUPS
- Classrooms for grades 4 and up

MATERIALS
- roll of shelf paper, at least eight inches wide
- ruler
- markers
- tape or tacks to secure the paper to the wall

DIRECTIONS AND DISPLAY

For children more interested in history than symbols, a time line works well.

Attach six feet of shelf paper to a long wall. This allows for about three inches per story. Draw a horizontal line with a bold marker, with a two-inch vertical line protruding from this line every three inches. There should be twenty-three of the vertical lines, with the twenty-fourth, the one that represents Christ, at the end.

Read a story and put the corresponding names in order on the line. The main character's name, the Scripture citation, or symbols can be used, keeping space restrictions in mind. Using a variety of colors adds visual interest as the time line progresses. When all the stories have been read and the name or symbol of Christ is added at the end of the line, add an arrow extending from the existing line and write the names of the children involved. This is a concrete way for them to see that they, too, are part of Christ's lineage.

Three-dimensional decorations

AGE LEVEL FOR CREATING THIS
Ages 3 to adult

TYPES OF GROUPS
- parish Advent workshop
- families
- groups with various ages

MATERIALS
- scissors
- tape
- rulers
- sewing needles and thread
- pens, markers, crayons
- staplers
- ribbons, streamers
- various colors of tissue and construction paper
- pipe cleaners
- thin wire
- self-hardening clay
- craft sticks
- felt and fabrics scraps
- glue and glitter glue (white and colored)
- glitter and glitter pens
- fabric paints
- sequins, buttons, etc.
- sturdy tree for display, such as a deciduous tree branch secured in a bucket of sand or an undecorated Christmas tree

DIRECTIONS AND DISPLAY
This method is perhaps the most enticing to those with artistic abilities. After reading a story, provide participants with materials. Provide lots of time, perhaps some snacks, and plenty of room for creativity. The symbols created will vary as greatly as the number of participants and will make a delightful display.

Medallion tree

AGE LEVEL FOR CREATING THIS
Ages 8 to adult

TYPES OF GROUPS
- parish teen or preteen groups
- families with elementary-aged or older children

MATERIALS
- self-hardening pottery clay
- waxed paper
- rolling pin
- table knives
- three-inch jar covers or round cookie cutters
- rounded toothpicks
- trays for drying
- thin ribbon of various bright colors
- sturdy branch or tree

DIRECTIONS AND DISPLAY
The medallions take time to make, and then need some days to dry and harden. Gather to create them a few weeks before Advent begins. After Christmas, pack the medallions carefully away for next year.

Work on waxed paper on a smooth surface. Roll out self-hardening clay as you would cookie dough, to a 1/8-inch thickness. Cut into circles. With a toothpick, draw a symbol for each story into the clay, taking care not to push the toothpick all the way through. Use symbol suggestions (page 83) or the provided symbols (pages 84-95) for inspiration. The name of the story character can also be added near the bottom. At the top center, make a hole through the clay large enough for a thin ribbon to be pushed through. Allow the medallions to dry away from a heat source, turning them daily. They will dry in three to four days. Pull colorful ribbon through the hole on each one.

After you share each story, have a child ceremoniously hang the medallion on the tree.

Felt banners

AGE LEVEL FOR CREATING THIS

Ages 7 and up, and at least one adult is needed

TYPES OF GROUPS

- parish family event
- elementary classrooms
- families at home

MATERIALS

FOR THE BANNER:

- felt fabric in a neutral color, measuring 28" x 36"green felt for the tree, measuring at least 25" in length and 23" in width
- several inches of brown, black, or tan felt for the tree trunk
- fabric scissors
- pencils
- ruler
- glue
- a needle and thread or a sewing machine
- a half-inch-thick dowel thirty inches long

FOR THE SYMBOLS:

- Felt squares and pieces in various colors (red, blue, purple, yellow, gold, black, green lighter than the tree felt, pink, tan, brown, etc.)
- sequins
- "eyes," such as for a stuffed animal, but very small; purchase at a craft store
- glitter
- markers
- safety pins or Velcro Hook and Loop if necessary
- fabric scissors and small embroidery-type scissors

DIRECTIONS AND DISPLAY

This can become a family or parish treasure.

To make the banner: fold over two inches along the top edge of the large sheet of felt to form a casing, and stitch. With green felt, cut an evergreen tree shape. A tree that is 25" tall and 23" at the widest point will fit onto this size banner. With a brown, black, or tan felt piece, cut a trunk. Glue or stitch the tree and trunk onto the banner. Slip a dowel into the casing.

To make the symbols: use felt pieces and fabric scraps of varying colors to fashion small symbols for each story. These can be made in the actual shape of the symbol or be glued onto a felt base. Heavier symbols may need a bit of Velcro Hook and Loop sewed onto the back, or to be pinned to the banner with a safety pin. Lighter symbols will just adhere to the felt.

A Jesse Tree booklet

AGE LEVEL FOR CREATING THIS

Ages 7 and up

TYPES OF GROUPS

- Elementary classes in day schools or religious education classes
- Families

MATERIALS

- Notebooks (or use individual sheets of paper and bind with yarn at the end of Advent)
- pencils or pens
- markers or crayons

DIRECTIONS AND DISPLAY

- After listening to the story, participants rewrite it in their own words. They also may choose to illustrate the story in any way they wish.

As this method does not create a visual focus, consider using it with another method, particularly one that has been completed prior to Advent, such as the Medallion Tree.

Inside the stories

Preceding each story, you will find this information:

Based on: This gives the location in Scripture where you will find this story.

Why is this story/person on the Jesse Tree?: This is a brief explanation of why the characters or the story are especially important in Jesus' lineage.

Reading this story: This offers suggestions on audience participation or other suggestions for the presentation of some of the stories.

Listener's guides: Teachers may choose to use these guides to help listeners focus on the story. They are a list of questions, some for grades kindergarten through 3, and others for grades 4 through 8. The answers can all be found very specifically in the story.

Family and other group discussions: These discussion suggestions go deeper into the story than the Listener's guides. They offer insight into characters or the historical settings, examining how the theme is reflected in today's world. They also provide challenges to decide how the listeners themselves might react to the story situation, etc. Use with groups that include adults and children, or for middle school students.

Prayer: While just listening to the stories is a form of prayer, a very brief prayer is included that is based on the story's theme.

Reflections for the storyteller: This is to encourage the storyteller to take a moment of quiet reflection before presenting the story.

Shorter Version: This book is used by people representing a wide range of ages. For longer stories, shorter versions are provided to be used with the youngest listeners.

THE STORIES

The story of Creation
Based on Genesis 1:1–2:4

Why is this story on the Jesse Tree?
- Most cultures have a creation story. The story presented here is, of course, the biblical one.

Reading this story
This is a wonderful story for a dramatic reading. Speak softly, then more loudly for effect. Involve your listeners by encouraging them to chant the lines, "That was the first day," etc. A simple signal, such as holding up the appropriate number of fingers to indicate which day, lets children know when to join in.

Listener's guides
FOR GRADES KINDERGARTEN THROUGH 3

- What is the very first thing God makes in this story?
- Name the three kinds of lights in the sky.
- What did God do on the seventh day?

FOR GRADES 4 THROUGH 8
- What does God call the great space over the water?
- On two different days light is created. Which days?
- Name three kinds of animals not mentioned in this version of the Creation story.
- What was created on the sixth day?

Family and other group discussions
- Does the Catholic Church teach that God created the world in seven days?
- How can this story enhance our appreciation for nature? How might it teach us about the need for good environmental stewardship?
- Why do you think the story ends with God resting on the seventh day? Connect the concept of a Sabbath with God's day of rest.

Prayer
Dear God, our Creator, thank you for the light, the dark, the mountains, and the deep seas! Thank you for the animals of the waters, the land, and the air! Thank you for the grasslands, the rainforests, the mountains, and the forests! And thank you for the delightful diversity of all your peoples in your great Creation! Amen.

Reflections for the storyteller
The first story for the Jesse Tree is set in the most ancient of times. It gives us a way to think symbolically about how the world and its order came to be. While many cultures have creation stories, the Israelites' version centered not just on the actual creation of the universe, but on God's love and involvement. Creation is the first saving act of God; it is God's pledge to the future. To the Israelites, saved from slavery in Egypt, the creation story illustrated why God intervened for them. They could

look at the mercy God had shown them and know that this was not the first time—and they believed that it would not be the last time. Through the creation story, God's love and mercy could be traced back, before Abraham and Sarah, even before Noah.

The Story

LONG, LONG AGO, in a time before time, there was God, the Creator. There were no sounds, no colors, no laughter. There was only darkness over the deep, and God's spirit hovered over the water.

God said, "Let there be light."

Brilliant light burst forth, piercing the darkness! God saw that the light was good, and separated it from the darkness. God called the light "day" and the dark "night."

That was the first day.

God said, "Let there be a great space above the waters." A space formed wide and blue, stretching over the waters. God called the space "sky."

That was the second day.

God said, "Let dry land appear." The waters moved over, gushed away, and rushed forward until land came forth, forming mountains, prairies, deserts, and forests. Trees, grasses, and flowers graced these places. God called the land "earth" and the waters "seas." And God saw that it was good.

That was the third day.

God said, "Let there be lights in the sky." In the blueness of the sky, a fiery ball appeared, which was the sun. At night, the pearly, paler moon appeared, and stars danced across the darkness.

That was the fourth day.

God said, "Let the waters be filled with fish." Then, large sleek fish, small quick ones, multicolored ones, and softly hued ones swam the seas.

God said, "Let the air be filled with birds." The sky was blessed with the songs and flight of millions of birds, and the trees were adorned with their nests.

That was the fifth day.

God said, "Let there be other animals." Lumbering, mooing cows appeared, along with scampering squirrels, slithering snakes, quick lizards, graceful deer, prowling cats, howling wolves.

God then said, "Let there be humankind." And God created humans, male and female. They emerged from the love of God, radiant and beautiful, for they were made in God's image. God saw all that was now created, and indeed, it was very good.

That was the sixth day.

On the seventh day, God rested.

The story of Adam & Eve
Based on Genesis 3

Why are these people on the Jesse Tree?
- Adam ("soil" and "man") and Eve ("life") are part of the biblical creation story.

Listener's guides

FOR GRADES KINDERGARTEN THROUGH 3
- At first, Eve and Adam could not get cold, sick, or _____.
- When Eve was walking, what animal did she meet?
- What did Adam and Eve eat?

FOR GRADES 4 THROUGH 8
- Describe the garden Eve and Adam first lived in.
- What was the only rule given to them by God?
- What animal did Eve meet?
- What would Eve and Adam learn if they ate the fruit?
- Name two things that happened after they ate the fruit.
- Describe what life was like outside the garden.

Family and other group discussions
- Why do you think this story exists? What do you think are the messages the original storytellers were trying to teach?
- What is the difference between trying to be like God and trying to be your own god?
- Is it important to know the difference between good and evil?

Prayer

Dear God our Creator, we live in a world that is both good and bad. We are people who can choose which way we will be. Please help us to live as Jesus taught so that we will make the right choices. Amen.

Reflections for the storyteller

How did life come to be as it is? There is so much beauty in life, yet there is much pain. So often there is laughter and there are also overwhelming difficulties. Why? This is a question people ask in each generation, for it is part of being human. One way to look for understanding is through stories.

Genesis 2 and 3 tell the stories of Adam and Eve and the Fall. Like the creation story, these are a reflection of the Israelite people's experience of God. The authors were trying to portray how sin began, and how it flows into history, changing the human condition from a pure to a fallen state. These stories sketch characters with which every reader can identity.

The name "Adam" comes from a pun on the Hebrew word "adamah," meaning "soil" and "man." It can refer to one man, but often is used as a collective term for humankind. Eve appropriately means "life" or "to live."

Most cultures have lore involving something forbidden. The protagonist disobeys this rule and thereby changes the right order of things. In this story, eating the fruit was an abuse of freedom, and so Adam and Eve were turned out of the Garden of Eden. Thus the unhappiness and sin of the world began. Adam and Eve had chosen to become their own god, thus causing what seemed to be a permanent separation from God, the source of all life. Without God, death, sorrow, and sin resulted. But while the story of the Fall teaches that sin is plentiful, it sets the stage for salvation and for Christ's coming. Sin does abound, but so does God's love.

The Story

EVE AND ADAM, THE FIRST WOMAN AND MAN, lived in the garden God had made for them. There were trees with sweet fruits to eat, and gentle animals roamed the land. It was neither too hot nor too cold. The first woman and man did not work nor did they get sick or hurt. God gave them everything they needed, and they were happy.

God did say they were not to eat the fruit from one certain tree in the middle of the garden. They were not to touch it, or they would die. Everything else they could eat. That was the only rule.

One day, Eve was out walking and she met the snake. Now Snake was a clever animal, and knew how to play tricks.

Snake asked, "Did God really say you can't eat from the fruits of that tree?"

Eve looked around. "We can eat from any of the trees. I especially love that fruit, over there," she said, pointing to a fig tree.

Snake waited. Eve went on, as the snake knew she would.

"There is only one fruit we cannot eat, from that tree," she said, pointing. "We are not even to touch it. If we do, we will die."

Snake chuckled. "No, you'll not die! You were told that because God knows that on the day you eat it, you will be like a god. You'll understand good and evil."

Good and evil? Be like God? Eve pondered this as she walked over to the forbidden tree. She wanted to understand more things. If the snake was right, maybe this fruit would help her.

Snake watched silently as Eve stood under the tree. She touched the tree's bark. She peered at the fruit. It looked as good as any other fruit she had eaten, perhaps better. It was beautiful. She glanced around. No one was looking, at least as far as she could tell.

She reached up, then stopped as she heard Adam's footsteps. She looked at Adam, then again reached up, plucking the fruit from the tree. She took two, one for herself and one for Adam.

They each took a bite.

And nothing was ever the same again.

Eve and Adam both gasped.

They realized that they were naked! Quickly they took the leaves from a fig tree and fashioned clothing to cover their bodies.

Suddenly they heard the sound of God walking in the garden.

Eve and Adam then did something they had never done before: they hid. They had a feeling that was new to them: shame.

God asked, "Where are you? I have heard your voices. Adam?"

Adam called out from his hiding place, "I was afraid because I didn't have any clothes. So I hid."

"Who told you that was wrong? Have you been eating the fruit I told you not to eat?"

"It was Eve!" Adam exclaimed. "She gave me the fruit, and I ate it."

"Eve, what have you done?"

From her hiding place Eve protested. "The snake tempted me, so I ate it."

"For this, you will now know pain and unhappiness," God said. "You will work hard for your food. Children will not come to you easily, but only through pain. You will have discomforts, you will know sickness, and you will someday die."

Then Adam and Eve lost their feelings of peace and harmony. They were given animal skins for clothing and sent out of the garden. No more could they eat without working. No more would they have only laughter and joy.

Outside of the garden, Eve shivered. It was the first time she had felt cold. Adam, who was always naming things, said, "This feeling—let's call it 'cold.'"

Then he looked at Eve, and there were tears on her cheeks.

"And this feeling—let's call it 'sad.'"

So, now, cold and sad, they stopped and looked back to the garden. There a magnificent cherubim stood guarding the entrance to the garden. They would never get back in again.

Ahead of them, the ground was covered with thistles and brambles. Together they looked around at the barrenness.

What, Eve wondered, would they do now?

The story of Noah
Based on Genesis 6:5–9:17

Why are these people on the Jesse Tree?
- Noah's son Shem is listed in the genealogy of Jesus in the Gospel of Luke.

Listener's guides

FOR GRADES KINDERGARTEN THROUGH 3
- Noah's family was on the ark because of a 1) tornado 2) flood 3) hurricane.
- Name three kinds of animals in the story.
- What was the sign God put into the sky? Draw this sign.

FOR GRADES 4 THROUGH 8
- Name five kinds of work that Noah and his family did to prepare for the flood.
- What was the pitch used for?
- Where did they get the pitch?
- How many decks were on the ark?
- How many days did it rain?
- What was the sign God put into the sky? What did it mean?

Family and other group discussions
- Imagine you are Noah's child. What do you think as you build a huge boat and put animals on it?
- What were the reactions of onlookers? What do you think they said?
- Have we ever chosen to do something that other people wouldn't do?
- Noah's family sang, told stories, and prayed together. What kinds of things do we do as a family/parish?
- Have you seen an image of a dove with a small branch with leaves in its mouth? Based on this story, what do you think that image means?

Prayer

Dear God, our Creator, you gave us the monkeys, spiders, giraffes, bees, crocodiles, and other animals. You gave us the clouds, the trees, the rain, and the soil. You who gave us all of life, please give us wisdom to live this life with care, respect, and dignity. Amen.

Reflections for the storyteller

Noah may have been a tent dweller and a skilled craftsman. Faithfully following the ways of God, Noah was a man of integrity in an unjust world. Creation had been very good when God created it, but by Noah's time wickedness had taken over the earth. God chose to destroy everything in order to preserve what was right, and then use it to start over. Only Noah and his family and some animals were chosen to survive the great flood.

The Story

PART ONE

THE GRAPE VINES GREW STRONG AND VIGOROUS. Noah ambled in his vineyard, humming happily as he inspected the plants. Nearby his daughter-in-law Deborah cradled her tiny son, Ashur. Deborah understood Noah's feelings. She too was thankful for all her blessings. Never again would there be a flood so vast they would need to take shelter in the ark! Now rains were only gentle, life-giving ones. God had promised.

She would never forget the day that Noah told them of the coming flood. The family saw his solemn, worried look and wondered uneasily. God had spoken to him, Noah explained. People had become so wicked they would soon perish in a great flood. Only Noah's family, who remained faithful to God, and some animals would survive. They were, God said, to build a huge boat, called an ark.

Noah and his wife, their sons Shem, Japheth, and Ham, and their wives built a large boat called an ark that was so towering it had three decks on it! The men toiled many long days sawing lumber, hammering, fitting. The women worked on the inside, smearing pitch from trees over every crack. It was filthy, hot, sticky work.

Outside, people watched as the ark slowly became the largest thing in town. The family seemed so foolish, working under a cloudless sky. A flood? Rain didn't even seem likely. Onlookers teased and jeered. Deborah dreaded this. Had Noah just imagined this message from God? Still, she worked beside her mother-in-law, spreading the pitch.

Next, they gathered their food, enough for many months. Bags of wheat and fruit filled corners of the awkward ark. They ran up and down the plank, lugging food, toting drinking water, carrying blankets and clothing while the sky remained cloudless.

Noah worked tirelessly. He never questioned God's directions. But the hardest work was yet to come.

"We must gather the animals," Noah told them. "We need to get a male and female of every kind. Of course we must also gather the kinds of food they need," Noah said.

The three brothers sighed. Was this even possible?

But God was with them and so it was. Little by little, the animals were found and brought to the ark. There were snakes, butterflies, tapirs, crocodiles, tigers, rabbits, parrots, bears, giraffes, opossums, just to start. Shem searched. Ham looked. Japheth explored. They brought back animals that bit, kicked or stung them, or tried to fly away from them. Deborah gathered grasses, nuts, and fruits that she hoped the animals would eat. How much did they need? She'd let God guide her.

Finally the animals were all together. Deborah paused to admire the touch of bright red on the blackbird's wing and the pattern on the zebra's back. The giraffe's neck was astounding! No wonder the ark needed to be so large!

What chaos as the family pushed, pulled, and coaxed the animals into the ark! The squawks and squeals, brays and neighs were deafening. The gangplank sagged under the weight of the elephants. Quickly it became slippery with animal droppings. Soon the inside of the ark would be as dirty. How would they ever live with the smell?

The wind picked up. Threatening clouds rolled in. Noah and his family walked up the plank together. It was God who shut the door.

At the sound, they paused. Some of the animals became frightened to be closed in, and the humans were afraid too. Already they heard the rain on the roof.

PART TWO

THE RAIN FELL AS IF IN BUCKETS, every day and every night. The constant drumming on the roof made it difficult to sleep. After several days the ark was floating. Feeding the animals, Deborah marveled that so much rain had fallen that the heavy ark was now afloat. Thank God they had put such great care into sealing it! It swayed now, and the animals seemed nervous. Deborah made soothing sounds as she fed the cowering rabbits, sang to the opossums, and stroked the sleek deer. Then she winked at the owls.

Even during the day, it was dark in the belly of the ark. But Noah's family remained cheerful, grateful to be saved. At meal times they prayed, told stories, and sang songs.

Ten days and nights of constant rain went by. Twenty days went by, and it still rained. Now the animals were drowsy from no exercise. The family was quiet. They had no heart for songs or stories. They prayed, but now it was a "help-us-God" kind of prayer.

Thirty-five days passed, thirty-nine days…then one night, the fortieth night, Deborah woke up. Shem was already awake. "Is something wrong?" she whispered.

"I don't hear the rain!" he whispered back.

She sat up, bewildered. After forty days and forty nights of rain, she had not recognized silence. "It's ended!" she whispered.

The whole family awoke. There were tears of joy and prayers of gratitude. At the first light, they crowded around the window. The water was so vast, the huge ark suddenly seemed small. And it held all of life that remained on the earth, like a seed floating on the water.

"Are we above the trees?" asked her sister-in-law.

"We are above the mountains!" Shem said.

They were silent then. It would be a long, long time before they could leave the ark.

Still, there was hope now! Deborah sang again as they scrubbed the top deck and hung wash. The clothing flapping in the breeze was a glad sight! The fresh air was such a pleasure they began eating their meals on that deck.

When the second deck was dry, they feasted there. Lizards skittered about now, and squirrels perched on roofs. Animal babies were born every hour. The noise and stench in the animals' quarters was overwhelming, but it was full of new life, and no one complained.

Days later, the water receded some, so Noah took a dove to the deck and let it go. As it soared into the air, Deborah's spirits rose with it. Never again would she take for granted the sight of a free bird in the sky! But it soon returned, having found nowhere to land.

Discouraged, they went back to their chores. A week later, Noah tried again, and the dove was gone for a long time.

"I see it! It's coming back!" Deborah called to the others. "It's bringing something!" The dove carried a fresh olive branch in its beak!

Another week passed, and again Noah sent the dove out. Everyone worked, but watched the deck where it might return. It never came back. The dove had found a new home on dry land!

Some weeks later God spoke, telling Noah it was time to leave the ark. Noah lifted the door and they gazed out onto dry land. The family said a thanksgiving prayer.

The animals swarmed out then, the large and the small, the awkward and the graceful. All had young with them. Deborah smiled. Smell and all, she had loved them.

She and Shem held hands as they descended from the ark. Within her, too, new life was stirring. Soon she would give birth, and her child would be born on the land.

And today, Deborah smiled at the baby as a light rain began to fall. Enjoying the mist on her face, she noticed the sun still shone a little. "Look!" she said to Noah. "A rainbow, just like the day we left the ark!"

Noah smiled. Taking the baby from her, he showed little Ashur the rainbow. "See the rainbow? It's God's sign that there will never be another great flood. It's God's covenant with us and with you and with your children and your children's children's children."

And the baby laughed and clapped his hands.

SHORTER VERSION

LONG, LONG AGO, the people of the earth turned their backs on God. Only Noah and his family were good and loving. God told Noah to build a huge, strong boat called an ark, and to find two of each kind of animal and take them onto the ark. Soon God would send a huge flood, and only Noah and his family and the animals on the ark would survive.

Noah's family worked hard to build the ark and even harder to catch the animals. Little by little, they filled the ark with two monkeys, spiders, zebras, giraffes, bees, tapirs, crocodiles, tigers, goats, squirrels, lizards, kangaroos, antelope, birds, bears, and all the other kinds of animals. Oh, the braying, chattering, barking, and howling that filled the ark!

Then the rain began to fall. It rained for forty days and forty nights. Noah fed all the animals. He cleaned up after them, and he tried to sleep. Each day, he hoped the rain would end soon.

Finally, all was quiet. The rain had stopped! Slowly, slowly, the water went down, and after many days, Noah was able to open the door. Out came the monkeys, spiders, zebras, giraffes, bees, tapirs, crocodiles, tigers, goats, squirrels, lizards, kangaroos, antelope, birds, bears, and all the other kinds of animals with their many babies. Out ran Noah and his family! And in the sky was a beautiful rainbow, a sign of God's promise that there would never again be such a terrible flood.

The story of Abraham

Based on Genesis 12:1-7; 15:1-6

Why is this person on the Jesse Tree?
- Abraham is the first leader of the people of Israel.
- He is considered the first of the patriarchs of the Jews and Christians.
- Abraham's story is the first glimpse of God's plan to show his love for people.
- Jews, Christians and Muslims are all descendants of Abraham.

Reading this story
While this is a short story, it contains a great deal about faith. Read it with both the sense of puzzlement and certainty Abraham must have felt.

Listener's guides
FOR GRADES KINDERGARTEN THROUGH 3
- What were Sarah and Abraham doing in the beginning of the story?
- What kind of housing did they have?
- Why did God tell Abraham to look at the stars?

FOR GRADES 4 THROUGH 8
- What kind of housing did Abraham and Sarah have?
- What does God ask of Abraham?
- _____ is the land they eventually come to.
- What is God's promise when they arrive?
- Why is Abraham puzzled by this promise?
- Why does God tell Abraham to look at the stars?

Family and other group discussions
- Abraham lived in a time when most people did not know of God in the sense that we do. Many invented gods and connected them with things that they believed had power over them. Why do you think they did this?
- In our time, are there "gods" in our culture? Do they have power over us?
- If you were Abraham, would you believe God's promise about having many descendants?
- Jews, Muslims, and Christians all claim ancestry to Abraham. Discuss what this means in terms of today's world.

Prayer
Like our ever-so-great grandfather, Abraham, we will try to be faithful to your ways, oh God, and wait for your blessings. Amen

Reflections for the storyteller
Abraham was the first of the great leaders whose family of faith is traced to Jesus. His name means "father," and he is known as the first of the patriarchs. All around him, others were worshiping gods of wood and clay, but Abraham was called by the real God, the God of Israel, to begin a new nation of believers. One of the most important characters in the Old Testament, Abraham teaches that God is calling us, and that our response should be love and trust.

The Story

OUTSIDE THE TENT, the flocks of sheep and herds of cattle were making noises with their animal voices. Servants moved through the groups of tents, going about their daily work. Nearby, beautiful, beloved Sarah kneaded bread. Abraham watched his wife and then looked out onto all that he owned. Yes, Abraham was a wealthy man in many ways.

He began to pray and heard the voice of God calling him.

"Abraham, leave this land of your parents and go to a land I will show you. I will make of you a great nation. I will bless you and those who bless you and curse those who curse you. All the communities of the earth shall find blessing in you."

Now Abraham was a faithful man. He loved God very much. If God asked him to leave this land he knew and move all the people and animals to an unknown place, Abraham knew he must go—no matter how hard it was.

So, sheep bleating, cows mooing, babies crying, tents folded, Abraham and Sarah's household began to move. When they reached the land of Canaan, God again spoke to Abraham: "To your descendants, I will give this land."

Abraham built an altar there, to honor God. But he was puzzled: what did God mean by his "descendants"? Abraham and Sarah had no children. Still, Abraham trusted God. His large group moved from time to time, and they met many other people and worked out various problems. They kept the ways of the Lord, and loved God.

A few years passed this way. One day, Abraham was again in his tent, praying. God appeared to him and said, "Fear not, Abraham, for I will reward you for all your faithfulness."

Despite this faithfulness, Abraham did ask God, "What good will your gifts be if I have no children? I keep your ways, I pray, I try to do as you ask. But if Sarah and I have no children, how can we pass on your blessings?"

God told Abraham to go outside. The night was cool. It was cloudless, and the sky was strewn with stars.

"Look up, Abraham!" God said. "Count the stars."

Abraham knew he could not count all the stars in that magnificent sky.

"All those stars will be the number of your descendants."

The night was quiet, the stars shone overhead. Abraham knew that nothing is impossible with God. He must be content to wait to see what God's plan was for him.

The story of Sarah

Based on Genesis 18:1-15; 21:1-7

Why is this person on the Jesse Tree?
- With her husband Abraham, Sarah helped establish the Jewish people.
- She is the mother of Isaac, a patriarch of the Jewish and Christian peoples.

Listener's guides
FOR GRADES KINDERGARTEN THROUGH 3
- Why was Abraham running?
- What did the visitors say about Sarah?
- Who do you think these visitors were?

FOR GRADES 4 THROUGH 8
- What time of day was it when this story took place?
- Why did Abraham run?
- What did Abraham ask Sarah to prepare?
- What did the stranger say about Sarah?
- How did Sarah react to this news?
- How is her reaction connected to the name chosen for the baby?

Family and other group discussions
- Who do you think were Abraham's visitors? Read Hebrews 13:2 and speculate.
- Abraham and Sarah offered hospitality to strangers. What do the Scriptures tell us about being hospitable? See Genesis 19:2-3; 24:31; Leviticus 19:34; Acts 28:2; Romans 12:13; 1 Peter 4:9.
- In this story, we hear, "Is there anything too wonderful for our God?" Think of times when something happened that is astounding and amazing.

Prayer
Thank you, God our Creator, for all the wonder and blessings! And thank you, too, for laughter! Amen.

Reflections for the storyteller
Sarah, Abraham's cherished and beautiful wife, traveled with him, enduring the hardships and uncertainty of this strange journey. Once she was taken from Abraham to become a wife of the Egyptian pharaoh. God intervened, and together she and Abraham left Egypt. But the greatest trial of Sarah's life was her inability to have children, for she lived in a society that looked down on women who did not have children. She resorted to having her handmaid, Hagar, give birth to Abraham's child, Ishmael. But God rewarded Sarah for her faithfulness, and joy and laughter came her way when she no longer expected it.

The Story

ALL WAS QUIET WITH ABRAHAM AND SARAH'S HOUSEHOLD, for they rested during the hottest part of the day. Even the animals felt drowsy. Sarah rested inside the tent, and Abraham sat just outside the door.

"Sarah!" Abraham called suddenly. "We are getting company!"

Peeking out, Sarah saw Abraham running towards three strangers. Who could they be? Why would they be traveling now, in this heat?

Abraham reached them, and bowed to the ground.

"I beg you kindly do not pass us by. I will have water brought to you, and we will share our bread with you before you go on," Sarah heard Abraham say.

The strangers agreed. Who would resist Abraham's hospitality? Sarah smiled as she watched Abraham hastening towards her. Now he would involve her.

She stepped away from the door and Abraham burst in. "Hurry! Make bread! We have company!" he exclaimed excitedly. "I'll go and see to the other arrangements."

He hastened off to have a servant prepare meat, and he gathered cream and milk. Sarah calmly mixed and stirred. Her hands covered with flour, she stayed in the tent, but listened as Abraham and the three guests settled into the shade near the tent.

"Where is your wife, Sarah?" one guest asked.

Sarah paused. How did this stranger know her name?

"In the tent," Abraham said. "She is preparing bread for us."

"I will visit you this time next year, and Sarah will have a son," the guest said.

Astounded, Sarah stopped kneading the bread dough. She was to have a baby? For years she had longed for a child, but now she was too old. She felt bewildered and then skeptical. It wasn't possible! The idea was so absurd, Sarah laughed softly to herself.

"Why did Sarah laugh and say 'am I really to have a child now that I am too old?'" the stranger asked Abraham.

Sarah put her floury hands to her mouth. Had she spoken out loud? No! Who was this stranger who knew miraculous things? Who was he that he knew her thoughts?

"Is anything too wonderful for God?" the stranger said. "At the same time next year, you and Sarah will have a son."

Now fear flooded Sarah. Was Abraham speaking to an angel? To God? Frightened, she called out, "I did not laugh!"

And the stranger replied, "Oh, yes you did!"

But God was not angry with Sarah for laughing, but looked kindly upon her. Within the year, Sarah, in her old age, gave birth to a baby boy.

They were inspired by God to name him Isaac, which means "May God laugh in delight." Sarah laughed joyfully, saying, "God has given me cause to laugh! All those who hear of this will laugh with me!"

And Abraham and Sarah rejoiced in their son, and taught him the ways of the Lord.

The story of Jacob
Based on Genesis 25:19-28; 27:1-29; 28:10-22

Why is this person on the Jesse Tree?
- Jacob is the third patriarch of the Jewish and Christian peoples, following his grandfather Abraham and father Isaac.
- Jacob is the father of the men who founded the twelve tribes of Israel.

Listener's guides
FOR GRADES KINDERGARTEN THROUGH 3
- Where was Jacob going?
- What did Jacob use for a pillow?
- What was Jacob's name for the place where he slept?

FOR GRADES 4 THROUGH 8
- What had Jacob done to his brother and father?
- What was Jacob's twin's name? What was he like?
- What did Jacob see in his dream? Who spoke to him in this dream?
- What does God rename Jacob?
- What does it mean?

Family and other group discussions
- Many sources say the meaning of the name "Jacob" is "supplanter." Does this fit Jacob at times? Jacob is eventually renamed "Israel" by God. How is that name used today?
- This is a challenging story. Discuss: do the ends justify the means? Can a person do something wrong and make it right again? Can Jacob do this?

Prayer
Dear God, like Jacob, our lives are complicated. Please help us to feel your presence and make the right decisions. Amen.

Reflections for the storyteller
When Isaac was of marriageable age, Abraham sent a servant back to the land of his birth to find a wife for his son. Through God's help, the servant found Rebekah. As with Isaac's parents, much time passed before they became parents. Rebekah carried twin boys, Esau and Jacob, who fought inside her even before she gave birth. God told Rebekah that these babies would someday become leaders of two countries, and that the second-born twin would be master over his brother.

Conflict and deception caused Jacob to flee his homeland. On this journey, Jacob encountered God, who pledged to Jacob what was promised to his grandfather Abraham years before. And, like his grandfather, Jacob accepted God as his god, worshiping and following the one true God of Abraham and Isaac.

The Story

THE SUN WAS SLIPPING FROM THE SKY. Jacob could not reach his uncle's house before nightfall. Thoughts of home, especially the last three days there, weighed on him. He pushed on. Jacob had tricked his father and his brother. It had been his mother's idea. She wanted Jacob to have their father's blessing so he would have the power to lead the family when Isaac died. Together they had confused the nearly blind, elderly Isaac into thinking Jacob was really Esau. Isaac gave Esau's blessing to Jacob. Esau was so angry he had threatened to kill Jacob. Now Jacob was journeying all alone, fleeing from Esau, heading for his Uncle Laban's home.

When he was a child, Jacob had heard his mother tell how he and his twin brother had fought even in her womb. Esau came first. Jacob, arriving just minutes later, had been clutching his brother's heel. Jacob had been trying to catch up to Esau ever since. They had nothing in common. Esau loved to hunt and was often off with his quiver and bow, bringing home the delicious wild game that their father, Isaac, enjoyed. Jacob was quieter and stayed home, working with the domestic animals. Yet now Jacob was on the road, and Esau was comfortably at home.

It grew dark. Jacob ate a cold dinner and looked for a good place to sleep. There was a pile of stones nearby. He took one and lay down, using the rock for a pillow. He pulled his cloak around him and fell asleep

Soon he was dreaming. Jacob saw a ladder standing on the ground, but the top of the ladder reached up and up, into the heavens! But this was no empty ladder. There were angels of God going up and down the steps! Jacob watched these beautiful figures moving gracefully.

Then, he dreamed he saw God standing over him, saying, "I am the Lord, the God of Abraham and the God of Isaac. I will give to you and to your children and grandchildren the land that you lay on now. Your descendants will be so many they will be like the specks of dust on the ground. These people will spread to the west and the east, to the north and to the south. Know that I am with you. I will keep you safe wherever you go, and bring you back to this land, for I will not desert you."

Jacob sat up. The dream was gone, but the feeling remained. "What a holy place this is!" Jacob thought. "Surely God is here and I never knew it! This is a house of God!" At the first hint of dawn, Jacob got up. He took the stone he had used for a pillow and set it up to be a monument to God. Taking oil from his pack, he slowly poured some over the stone, saying, "I name this place Bethel, the house of God."

Then, kneeling, he vowed to trust in God.

Pulling on his cloak, Jacob set off again. In time, he would meet God face to face, and God would rename him Israel, meaning "God rules." But for now, he was Jacob, moving with certainty toward his future, for he knew God would be with him.

The story of Leah and Rachel
Based on Genesis 29; 30:1-24; 35:16-20

Why are these people on the Jesse Tree?
- Leah and Rachel are nieces of Rebekah and Isaac, and wives of Jacob.
- They become the mothers of twelve sons, whose descendants become the twelve tribes of Israel, of whom Jesus is a descendant.

Reading this story
As this is the story of two sisters, it is best read in two voices.

Listener's guides
For grades Kindergarten through 3
- What are the names of the two sisters?
- Which one was the eldest?
- After many years, Jacob takes his family and goes back to where he grew up. Why did he do this?

For grades 4 through 8
- Why did Jacob come to live with his uncle and family?
- Why did he and Leah get married?
- Each sister had a sadness. Name these.
- What was the name of Rachel's firstborn son?
- Jacob had twelve sons. How many were Leah's children?

Family and other group discussions
- What is different about Jacob's marriages from marriage today?
- What does the word "deception" mean? What were the big deceptions in Jacob's life?
- There are many things about brothers and sisters in the story of Jacob and in this story. How do Leah and Rachel work out their differences? What happens with Jacob and his brother, Esau? Do you expect there might be difficulties amongst Jacob's children?

Prayer
Dear Jesus, as we prepare for your coming, we read of Rachel and Leah, a story that speaks of life being good and bad. Please help us learn to appreciate the good in life even when it is difficult to see. Amen.

Reflections for the storyteller
In Genesis, the emphasis is often on God's promise made to the patriarchs Abraham, Isaac, and Jacob, who were chosen to create a people of God. Of course, the women who shared their lives often had fascinating stories themselves. Leah and Rachel, two sisters who both became Jacob's wives, led bittersweet lives, but gave to the world the twelve men who led the twelve tribes of Israel. They are the matriarchs of the House of Israel.

The Story

Leah: I am Leah, the older of two sisters, cousin of Jacob and Esau. I remember the day, long ago, when Jacob came to our home. There was much excitement that day! He had left his parents, Isaac and Rebekah, and his twin brother, Esau, to come live with us.

Rachel: I am Rachel, the younger sister. I too remember Jacob's arrival. He was fleeing, for he had angered his brother. He noticed me right away. He had not been with us long before I knew Jacob loved me and I him.

Leah: I could see Jacob's love for Rachel, and I was bewildered. I knew our father Laban wanted Jacob to marry into our family, and, as the older sister, I must marry first. How would our father resolve this? When I learned his decision, I protested. No! This will not be a good solution! But my father never heard my protests.

Rachel: *(looking into the distance:)* Oh Jacob, my husband, the deception there has been in your life! First you deceived your father and brother; then, my father deceived you on your wedding day! *(To the audience:)* Jacob asked my father if he could marry me. My father said yes, but when it was time for the wedding, it was Leah, covered in a veil, who married Jacob. I, who loved him, stayed behind in my father's house and cried for my loss.

Leah: What could I do? I knew Rachel was heartbroken, but what about me? I will never forget Jacob's face when the morning light came and he realized he was married to me and not to Rachel. I will never forget the shock, the disappointment, the anger…

Rachel: Jacob came to my father's house in a rage. My father calmly told him he could marry me too, if he continued to work for him. Jacob and I were married some years later, but I must forever share my husband with my sister.

Leah: Rachel and I had always loved one another, but it was hard for me, knowing that Jacob loved her, and not me. It was a great comfort, then, when I realized I was carrying my first child.

Rachel: How happy Leah was then, and I was glad for her. But as she held her beautiful new son, Reuben, I must admit, I felt jealous.

Leah: God blessed me with sons, perhaps because I was not blessed with Jacob's love. Rachel and I had our family, wealth, food, but neither of us had what we really longed for.

Rachel: Babies, beautiful babies! My sister had Simeon, then Levi. She had more children, and I was envious. Then finally, the merciful God sent me a son! Joseph! My joy!

Leah: How Jacob doted on Joseph! It was hard on my children to see their father so taken with this new baby. But still, I was glad for Rachel. When she was carrying her second child, we began our journey.

Rachel: After all these years, Jacob wanted to return to his home and make up with his brother, Esau. As we got closer to Jacob's home, Esau came to greet us.

Leah: He had forgiven Jacob. All was well, for awhile…then Rachel went into labor. I got help, for I could see it would be a difficult birth. For hours Rachel labored, I grew more and more con-

	cerned, then alarmed. I knew Rachel was slipping away from us. The child was finally born, a boy, and she said to me:
Rachel:	I name him Ben-oni, son of my sorrow. Take care of him, Leah.
Leah:	And then, my sister, my lifelong companion, died as I cradled her son. Our other children played outside. They would grow up and have children of their own. We would become a strong family dedicated to God. And Rachel and I—it was our love and our sacrifice that helped bring this great family into being.

SHORTER VERSION

Jacob arrived at the home of his uncle, Laban. He had left his mother, Rebekah, his father, Isaac, and his twin brother, Esau, a few days before. Laban's whole family welcomed him.

The older daughter, Leah, knew her father wanted Jacob to marry into their family. Right away, she saw that Jacob liked her younger sister, Rachel. As it was the custom that the oldest daughter would marry first, she wondered how her father would solve this.

At that time, the laws said that a man could marry two or more women. Laban had Jacob first marry Leah, and then Rachel.

Leah and Rachel were sisters who loved each other. But Leah was sad that Jacob didn't love her. And Rachel was sad because she did not have a baby, while Leah had many babies.

After a few years, Rachel finally had a baby, a boy named Joseph. Then Rachel had one more baby named Benjamin. There were twelve sons in all. Like their mothers and father, and their great-grandparents Sarah and Abraham, they would grow up knowing and loving God.

The story of Joseph
Based on Genesis 37–46

Why is this person on the Jesse Tree?
- Joseph is the great-grandson of Abraham and Sarah, grandson of Isaac, and son of Jacob and Rachel.
- He leads his large family to years of safety and prosperity in Egypt.

Reading this story
The story of Joseph and his eleven brothers is one of sibling rivalry taken to the extreme. Because this is a topic familiar to many children, explore the listeners' views of Joseph and his brothers with discussion questions provided within the story.

Listener's guides
FOR GRADES KINDERGARTEN THROUGH 3
- What is Joseph's special piece of clothing?
- Joseph told the pharaoh there would be ____ years of hunger.
- What did the brothers come to buy from Joseph in Egypt?

FOR GRADES 4 THROUGH 8
- What dreams did young Joseph have about his brothers?
- Which of Joseph's brothers tried to protect him?
- Describe the dream that worried Pharaoh.
- What happens years later that causes Joseph's dreams about his brothers to become real?
- How does Joseph react emotionally when he sees his brothers after many years?
- Who did the brothers bring to Egypt after they met Joseph again?

Family and other group discussions
- Use the discussion questions within the story.

Prayer
Dear Jesus, you teach us to forgive one another. Help us to be forgiving like Joseph. Amen.

Reflections for the storyteller
Rachel's son Joseph was his father's favorite, but he was destined to leave Jacob to bring the people of Israel into Egypt, where they would further realize God's plan and love for them. Joseph's story is a complicated one, for he was a prophetic man and a wise leader.

The Story

THE OLDER SONS OF JACOB WERE IN THE FIELD TAKING CARE OF THE SHEEP when they saw Joseph coming.

Joseph, their father's favorite. Joseph, wearing the beautiful coat their father had given him. Joseph, who had dreams in which the brothers bowed down to him. Joseph, the brother they envied, the brother they hated.

He ran up to them, handsome in his coat and glad to see them. "I had another dream last night!" he said excitedly.

That did it! They could not hear about any more bragging dreams. Two of the stronger brothers seized Joseph. Reuben, the eldest, was frightened. He was afraid they would kill Joseph.

"Throw him into that pit over there," Reuben quickly suggested, knowing he could easily rescue Joseph later. "Don't harm him." But first they took off Joseph's fine coat, and only then threw him into the pit. A caravan of merchants came along, and the brothers decided to sell Joseph as a slave to the merchants. The brothers thought, "Joseph is on his way to Egypt now. We are done with him!"

- *Why do you think Joseph's brothers were so angry with him?*
- *Have you ever been deeply angry with a brother or sister?*
- *What might be Joseph's feelings?*

Joseph worked as a servant in Egypt and he began telling other people what their dreams meant. When Joseph was a young man, the pharaoh had a dream that greatly disturbed him. He dreamed seven well-fed, healthy cows were swallowed up by seven sickly, thin cows. He called for Joseph to interpret the dream.

"There will be seven years of plenty, when the earth will produce more food than can be eaten. This will be followed by seven years of drought, when the crops will fail, and people will starve," Joseph explained.

The pharaoh decided to believe Joseph, and he also decided to put Joseph in charge of saving and storing the extra food, so the Egyptian people would not go hungry during the drought. Joseph was a smart man and a good leader. He did his job well, and when the seven years of plenty were over and crops were poor, just as Joseph predicted, the Egyptian people did not starve.

But the people in nearby countries were hungry. They heard Egypt had food and began coming there to buy some. The pharaoh put Joseph in charge of selling the food. He was doing this job, dressed in fine Egyptian clothing and sitting in a special chair, when eleven brothers came in to ask for food—eleven brothers who looked familiar!

Joseph's heart leaped for joy. Here were Reuben, Simeon, Levi, and the others. Here, too, was handsome Benjamin, his brother who had been born when their mother Rachel died. Now Benjamin was a man, and Joseph barely recognized him. He realized that none of his brothers recognized him either. There they were, bowing down to him, just as the dream had predicted years ago. Now these brothers who had sold him as a slave needed him to help them feed their families.

- *If you were Joseph, what would you do at this point?*
- *Have you ever been in a situation where you had to choose between forgiving a brother or sister or getting even?*

Joseph did not say who he was, and gave his brothers sacks of grain. But he instructed a servant to hide his own silver cup in Benjamin's grain. The brothers left happily with their food, but they were stopped and accused of stealing the cup. They were arrested and brought back to Joseph. Benjamin was terrified.

Now Joseph chose to explain. "I am Joseph, your brother," Joseph then told them, and he began to cry.

Amazed, bewildered, the brothers all stared at him, and of course they remembered how badly they had treated Joseph.

Still crying, Joseph told them not to be sorry. He said, "It was God's plan that I come to Egypt so I could save our family now. But tell me, is Jacob our father still alive?"

His brothers answered, "Yes."

Joseph was overjoyed! They must go home, Joseph instructed his brothers, and get their father, their wives, and children, and come back here to live with him. Joseph would see to it that they had enough food and they could all be a family once again.

It was a jubilant Jacob who traveled to Egypt with his family to join Joseph. The children, grandchildren, and great-grandchildren would all grow up there, in the land of the pharaoh.

- *Joseph was no longer angry with his brothers, but still, he tricked them. What do you think about this?*
- *Joseph believed that God had wanted him to go to Egypt. Have you ever had something unusual happen in your life that later seemed to be God's plan?*

SHORTER VERSION

ONE DAY, JOSEPH RAN TO HIS BROTHERS as they took care of sheep in the fields. "I had another dream where you all bowed down to me!" he said. It made them so angry he thought they were really going to hurt him! Then they noticed a group of traveling merchants who were nearby. Much to Joseph's horror, they sold him to these travelers!

He ended up in the country of Egypt. It wasn't long before Joseph's understanding of dreams got him a great job. The pharaoh, or king, had a dream that bothered him. Joseph was called in to tell the pharaoh what it meant. "There will be seven years when there is good weather and we will grow more than enough food. Then there will be seven years of bad weather—food won't grow and people will be hungry."

The pharaoh believed Joseph and decided to put him in charge of managing the food. During the good years, he had farmers saving the extra food. When the bad years came, Egyptians still had enough food. But people in other countries were hungry. They came to Egypt to buy food.

Guess who came to ask Joseph for food: his brothers! They had children now and all were hungry. Joseph could have been very angry at them. Because of his job, he could even have had them put into jail.

But Joseph forgave them. He was so glad to see them he cried, and then invited them to bring their families to Egypt to live. And, to Joseph's joy, his father, Jacob, was still alive! How happy Jacob and Joseph were to be together as a family again!

The story of Moses and Miriam

Based on Exodus 2:1-10; 14:15-16; 15:20-21; 16:1-3; 31:18

Why are these people on the Jesse Tree?
- Moses was the greatest of the Hebrew prophets.
- He brought the Jewish people out of slavery in Egypt.
- God gave Moses the Ten Commandments.
- Moses appeared to the apostles with Jesus at the Transfiguration.

Listener's guides
For grades Kindergarten through 3
- What did Miriam's mother put into the water?
- Who found the basket?
- What kind of bread did God give Miriam and Moses?

For grades 4 through 8
- Why did the basket not sink?
- When the basket was floating on the water, Miriam was reminded of _____'s _____.
- Who found the basket?
- Why was this dangerous for the baby?
- Only after ____ plagues would the pharaoh let the Israelites leave Egypt.
- What did Miriam do after the people were freed?
- Moses went up a mountain where God gave him the ____ _____.

Family and other group discussions
- Why do you think Moses is seen as the greatest of the Hebrew prophets?
- Do you know each of the Ten Commandments? What is their importance?
- Moses was not a good speaker (see Exodus 4:10). Yet God chose Moses for a tremendous and difficult job which would require much speaking. Discuss what this might have meant to Moses, and why God sometimes seems to choose people who don't seem to be right for a job.

Prayer
Dear God, Moses was faced with many frightening and hard challenges. Please help us to be brave and tenacious when we too face difficulties. Amen.

Reflections for the storyteller
The pharaoh of Egypt welcomed Joseph's large family with gifts, food, and land. Jacob was reunited with his son Joseph, and all led happy lives. Jacob was sometimes called Israel by God, and his family became known as the Israelites. Four hundred years passed, this family grew to a tremendous size, and the memory of Joseph's great success in saving Egypt from starvation had faded. The pharaoh of this time worried that the Israelites might become too powerful. So, he ordered the midwives to kill any boy children born to the Israelite women. And he made slaves of the people. Into this situation, the great leader Moses was born.

Moses is the central figure of the Old Testament, the great servant and mediator of God. His story is multifaceted. In many ways, Moses prefigures Christ: when each was a baby, a ruler set out to kill all the male infants of certain groups, but both Moses and Jesus were spared; Moses had climbed a mountain to receive the Ten Commandments and Jesus climbed a mountain for the Transfiguration and went up another mountain to proclaim his "sermon on the mount"; when Moses led the Israelites into the desert, God provided manna, a food often compared with the Eucharist; and the waters of Jesus' baptism are compared to Moses' saving waters, first when he was an infant floating in a basket, and later when he parted the sea for his people to escape.

The Story

THE WIND RUSTLED IN THE REEDS SURROUNDING THE RIVER. Miriam sat in the tall grasses, watching and waiting.

Just a few yards away floated a basket on the water's surface. It was a fine papyrus basket, woven by her mother's able fingers. She then lined it with bitumen and pitch, which would keep the water out, so the basket would not sink. Miriam watched it rock gently with the river's movement. She recalled the story of Noah's ark. The basket looked like she imagined the ark had looked. And like the ark, this basket too held precious life.

The silence of the morning was broken by voices. Miriam hunched smaller into the reeds and waited anxiously.

Several young women came down to the river bank to bathe. When Miriam saw who they were, her heart began to pound. One of them was a princess, the pharaoh's daughter—the very same powerful pharaoh who held her people, the Israelite people, in slavery! The same pharaoh who had declared that all their baby boys must be cast into the river and drowned!

And floating on this river in the papyrus basket lay Miriam's baby brother. Hoping to save him, her mother had placed her son in the basket to hide him by day at the river. Now he would be found by the pharaoh's daughter! Could it be worse? If he cried, yes. There was a chance if he did not cry. Oh, please, baby, Miriam pleaded silently, don't cry!

The voices filled the air, but soon Miriam heard the sound she most dreaded: the thin, unmistakable sound of a baby's cry.

"Where is that coming from?" the pharaoh's daughter asked, stopping her splashing and looking around.

Her attendants were silent, listening, and the baby's cries grew louder.

"It comes from over there—look! There is a basket! Bring the basket to me!" the princess said.

An attendant waded into the deeper water and drew the basket closer. The princess lifted the blanket and saw the baby. Miriam crept as close as she dared.

"Oh, this must be a child of one of the Israelites," said the pharaoh's daughter. "It must be hungry."

Miriam knew she must act if her brother was to be saved. Perhaps the princess was not as harsh as her father, the pharaoh. She stood up and approached the water's edge.

Gathering her courage, Miriam called, "Shall I go and find a woman who might feed the child?" Fear was betraying her voice.

Startled, the princess looked up at Miriam. Then she directed, "Yes, go."

Miriam waited to hear no more. Running, she reached her mother quickly.

When her mother, Jochebed, saw Miriam, she feared the worst. She cried out, "My baby!"

Miriam grabbed her mother's hand, explaining as they ran.

At the water's edge, the princess tenderly handed the crying baby to Jochebed. "Take this child and care for him until he is older. Then he can come to me," she instructed. "You will be paid as long as you have him." Then she looked at the baby once more, saying, "I will name you Moses, for I saved you from the water."

Miriam, Jochebed, and the baby went home. As the sun rose to its height in the noonday sky, Jochebed fed her baby. Miriam knew that some day her mother would have to present her little brother to the pharaoh's daughter, and he would be raised as an Egyptian. When the baby was content, Jochebed said, "I must return to work. Care for him, Miriam, for he is ours for a little longer."

Miriam held him close, and sang to him. He looked into her eyes as she sang.

Neither of them could know that years later, Moses would be called by God to become a great leader. God would speak to him through a burning bush, directing him to ask the pharaoh to set the Israelites free. Pharaoh would be so determined to keep them captive that he held firm through nine terrible plagues sent by God. He would only relent at the tenth plague, the death of all firstborn Egyptian sons. Moses would lead the people of Israel out of Egypt. And stubborn Pharaoh would change his mind and send hundreds of chariots and Egyptian soldiers to chase them, quickly gaining on them. At God's direction, Moses would stretch out his arm over the sea and the waters would part into two sections, leaving a path of dry land for the Israelites to escape. The waters would close back over the charioteers, and they would drown.

It would then be Miriam who would lead the people—in a song and dance of celebration once they were safely across.

But for now, Miriam could not know any of this as she held her baby brother. She only knew that the baby was alive and safe.

He would be allowed to grow up and serve God in a special way. Miriam would help her brother as he tried to keep the people of Israel faithful to God in the long years of desert living. She'd hear the complaints the people hurled at Moses when they were tired and hungry. She would stand by Moses when he called upon God to provide food and water for the people. She'd eat the bread called manna that God would send.

She would watch as Moses climbed a mountain where God would speak with him. She would wait below as God gave Moses the Ten Commandments and made a covenant with the Israelites. From then on they would be called God's chosen people.

Miriam would see the people, tired of waiting for Moses to come back down the mountain, turn to false gods. She'd see Moses' anger and sadness. Together Moses and Miriam would live for many years amid the fears and unhappiness of the Israelites. And for all those years, they would experience God's great love and care.

Life for Miriam and Moses would always be difficult, but filled with God's presence.

Today, in this Presence, the house was quiet, except for Miriam's lullaby.

SHORTER VERSION

ONCE THERE WAS A BABY NAMED MOSES. When he grew up he would do great things that were very hard for him. At that time, the Israelite people, the descendants of Jacob's sons, were forced to be slaves in Egypt. God wanted Moses to get the king, called Pharaoh, to let the people leave Egypt and be free once again. Over and over again, Moses had to talk to Pharaoh. Finally, he let them leave. Just when it seemed the hard part was over, Pharaoh sent to chase them hundreds of horses pulling chariots of soldiers! With God's help, Moses managed to save all the people. Then he spent the rest of his life helping them find the land they would call home.

But first, baby Moses had to grow up—and he almost didn't!

The pharaoh at that time decided there were too many Israelite people! He made a law that said all the baby boys must die! Moses' mother made a plan and then made a wonderful basket. She lined it with pitch from trees so no water could seep in. Here she placed her little son, and put the basket to float on a small part of the river. Here, she thought, no soldiers would find him. Her daughter Miriam hid, watching. No soldiers came, but the pharaoh's daughter did! She did not want this baby hurt, so she decided she would adopt him. Miriam said she knew someone who could take care of the baby. Of course, it was Moses' mother. Little Moses was saved so he could grow up and do all the amazing things God would need him to do.

The story of Ruth
Based on the book of Ruth

Why is this person on the Jesse Tree?
- Ruth was the great-grandmother of King David. Scripture says Jesus is from the "House of David."

Reading this story
Some of Ruth's words became particularly cherished Scripture verses. You might choose to have listeners join in on Ruth's often repeated words on faithfulness.

Listener's guides
FOR GRADES KINDERGARTEN THROUGH 3
- Who moves to Bethlehem with Naomi?
- How did Ruth get food for Naomi?
- Finish this sentence: Wherever you go, I _____ _____.

FOR GRADES 4 THROUGH 8
- What town did Naomi and family leave because of famine?
- From the description in the story, what do you think "gleaning" means?
- Name two ways Ruth provided food for Naomi.
- Fill in the blanks: Wherever you _____, I shall _____. Wherever you _____, I shall _____. Your _____ shall be my _____, and your _____ shall be my _____.
- What does Boaz hear about Ruth?
- This story has a happy ending. What part of the ending do you like best?

Family and other group discussions
- What are some ways a person can be faithful to another?
- If Ruth's great-grandchild is King David, who was her grandson? (Hint: this tradition is named after him.)
- What is gleaning? See Deuteronomy 24:19–22 or Leviticus 19:9–10. Then consider these concepts around gleaning:
    » This practice shows us that the seeds of Christian charity began centuries ago in the Jewish culture.
    » We are being told that as soon as we feel entitled to things, we must then think of others who have less.
    » Our personal blessings give us a responsibility socially.
- Imagine yourself picking up wheat in a field that harvesters have been through and how much you would need to pick up to make even one loaf of bread; then think of the expression "slim pickings."

Prayer
Dear Lord, show us how to be faithful to you as Ruth was to Naomi. Help us be generous with others as Boaz was to Ruth. Amen.

Reflections for the storyteller
Over a course of many years the Israelites settled in Canaan. This was the land Moses was leading

them to before his death, the land God had promised. There were times of war and times of famine, but also times of peace. In this period, Israel had no king, but there were leaders, servants of the Lord, who ruled temporarily. The book of Ruth is set during this period of history and echoes Israel's covenant with God. Ruth and Boaz are the great-grandparents of King David.

The names of Naomi's family members may be fictitious and chosen for their symbolism: Mahlon means "sickness," Chilion means "pining away," and Orpah means "she who turns away." Elimelech means "my God is king," Naomi means "my fair one," and Ruth means "the beloved."

The Story

THE BABY KICKED HIS CHUBBY LEGS AND HELD HIS ARMS OUT. Naomi picked him up, rubbed his back, and quietly sang a little chant:

Wherever you go, I shall go. Wherever you live, I shall live. Your people shall be my people, and your God shall be my God.

Happily rocking the baby to sleep, Naomi remembered how sad she had once been. Long ago, she had left this place called Bethlehem. There was a famine. Seeking food, she and her family traveled to the land of Moab and made their home there. Her husband Elimelech died, and her two sons, Chilion and Mahlon, also died soon after marrying. Naomi, unhappy and lonely, wanted to return to her home in Bethlehem, now that the famine was over.

But first she wanted to say good-bye to her daughters-in-law. This was their homeland, where they belonged. Orpah and Ruth cried, for they both loved Naomi very much. Then Orpah said good-bye and left to rejoin her family. Ruth, however, refused to go.

Naomi smiled as she remembered Ruth's quiet words:

Wherever you go, I shall go. Wherever you live, I shall live. Your people shall be my people, and your God shall be my God.

Naomi had been so sad and anxious to get back home that she had simply let Ruth come with her. They traveled together, Ruth protecting and helping Naomi. When they reached Bethlehem, people there were glad to see Naomi again and interested in meeting Ruth. But still, Naomi felt unhappy and bitter about all that had happened to her. At least now they had a place to live, in Naomi's old home, but they had very little to eat.

"Is it the custom in your country that the poor may glean the leftovers from the harvest?" Ruth asked Naomi.

Naomi answered, "If the landowner is kind."

Ruth left the house then, and Naomi watched her go, beginning to understand Ruth's words to her:

Wherever you go, I shall go. Wherever you live, I shall live. Your people shall be my people, and your God shall be my God.

Dear Ruth was going to provide food for them! Naomi, despite her sadness, turned her attention to creating a nice home for Ruth.

Ruth did the exhausting work of a gleaner. From dawn to dusk, she bent over in the fields, picking barley that was left behind by the harvesters. Slowly she filled a sack with the only food that she and Naomi would have after the harvest. When she returned home, her tired face shone.

"I have been met with kindness all day," Ruth said. "The owner of the field told the harvesters not to disturb me. I think he told them to purposely leave barley behind for me!"

"The God of Israel has been watching over you!" Naomi said.

"That is not all!" Ruth went on. "When the workers stopped to eat, the landowner called me to him. He offered me water and then he shared his bread with me! I asked him what I had done to deserve such kindness and he said—-"

Ruth paused and seemed embarrassed.

"Go on," Naomi insisted.

"He said he had heard that I had left my home and everything I knew to come here with you."

Naomi was stunned. All she could think about were Ruth's words:

Wherever you go I shall go. Wherever you live, I shall live. Your people shall be my people, and your God shall be my God.

Ruth was handing food to Naomi. "He shared so much food with me, I brought you some. Please eat."

Naomi said, "Blessed be this man! Do you know his name?"

"Boaz," replied Ruth.

Naomi stared at Ruth. "Boaz? Boaz! He is a relative of my husband! He was always a kind and generous man. We are blessed that he has taken such a liking to you!"

And they were indeed blessed, for Boaz had seen Ruth's faithfulness to Naomi, and now he offered Ruth his own faithfulness. Eventually they were married, and of course, Naomi went to live with them.

Now the baby in her arms was asleep. Naomi gently laid him down. Someday, this beautiful child of Ruth and Boaz would have a grandson who would become the greatest king of Israel. But for today, Naomi covered the baby with a blanket and whispered:

Wherever you go, I shall go. Wherever you live, I shall live. Your people will be my people, and your God shall be my God.

The story of Samuel

Based on 1 Samuel 1:1–11; 3:1–20

Why is this person on the Jesse Tree?
- Samuel was a member of the twelve tribes of Israel.
- He acts for God in choosing David to become king.

Listener's guides
FOR GRADES KINDERGARTEN THROUGH 3
- Why is Hannah sad?
- What did she name her child?
- Who called to Samuel?

FOR GRADES 4 THROUGH 8
- Why does Eli think Hannah has been drinking wine?
- What is Hannah's sadness?
- What does the name "Samuel" mean?
- Who does Samuel think is calling him at first?
- Who is actually calling him?
- What becomes of Samuel when he grows up?

Family and other group discussions
- Hannah wanted her son to serve God all his life. How do people in your family help children learn about God? Talk about what are the talents of people you know that might help them do God's work in the world.
- Imagine you are Eli. What might he have been thinking when Samuel was being called?
- What does the name "Samuel" mean? The name "Isaac" means laughter, because his mother Sarah laughed happily about having Isaac. What are the meanings of some names of people in your group? Do these meanings affect them?

Prayer
Speak, Lord, for like Samuel, we are listening. Amen.

Reflections for the storyteller
Samuel is an important figure of the Old Testament. He represents Israel's transition from a tribal confederation to a monarchy. He became the guardian of the sacred traditions—to keep Israel from abandoning its holy practices as it took on the ways of the world. A prophet, a priest, and the last judge, Samuel was a public figure among the twelve tribes. Like many other key characters, he began life as a longed-for child, the son of a woman who hoped and waited for years to be blessed with a child. And when Samuel was still a child, the guiding hand of God was clearly upon him.

The Story

ELI LOOKED UP TO SEE A WOMAN ENTER THE TEMPLE. There were tears on her cheeks, and though she was silent, her lips moved constantly. What was her problem? Eli wondered. He observed her more. She swayed a little as she continued to mouth soundless words.

She must have had too much wine! As priest of the temple, Eli would have none of that here! Old Eli rose stiffly and walked quietly up to her.

Before he could speak, the woman turned tearful eyes on him, and said, "Do not think ill of me. I am very unhappy, and so I pray with great sorrow. My name is Hannah, and I have no children. I am asking God to give me a son. If I could have a son, I would let the child live in the temple to serve God all his life."

Eli nodded, then smiled kindly and said, "Go in peace. May the God of Israel grant you what you have asked."

Sometime later, God answered her prayer. She and her husband became parents of a son, Samuel, which means "called by God." When Samuel was old enough, Hannah carried out her promise: she took him to the temple, where he stayed to live with Eli, serving God.

One night, young Samuel went to sleep as usual. Eli was also asleep. All was quiet. Samuel rolled over. He opened his eyes. Why had he awakened? There was no sound; nothing was amiss. Samuel yawned and closed his eyes.

Then he heard a voice, calling, "Samuel!" He sat up. Eli must need something.

"Here I am!" Samuel answered, and ran to Eli's bed.

Eli opened one eye just enough to see Samuel standing there, looking very drowsy.

"I didn't call you. Go back to sleep."

Samuel stumbled back to his bed. He must have been dreaming but it had seemed so real! But soon the boy was settled down again and slumbering soundly.

"Samuel!"

Wearily, Samuel trudged into Eli's room. "Here I am," he said. "You called me."

More awake now, Eli answered, "I didn't call you. Go back to sleep."

Puzzled, Samuel lay down, but soon the voice again called him. Once more, he went off to Eli's room. By this time, Eli was sitting up, unable to sleep. He had not heard any voice, but he knew that Samuel was not dreaming. Eli understood that God was calling the boy. "Go to sleep, and if you are called again, reply, 'Speak, Lord, for your servant is listening,'" Eli instructed.

Once more, Samuel headed to bed. He lay down, but soon he awoke to the voice, "Samuel, Samuel!"

"Speak, Lord, for your servant is listening," Samuel answered.

And God began speaking to Samuel. From that day on, God spoke to Samuel. Samuel told others what God said. Samuel became a great prophet, and served God all his life.

The story of David
Based on 1 Samuel 16; 17:1–50; Psalm 23

Why is this person on the Jesse Tree?
- David was the son of Jesse.
- David became a great king, and for centuries after, anyone who was an descendant could say he or she was "from the House of David." This is said of Jesus.

Reading this story
Psalm 23 has been set to music in a variety of ways. Find a version your listeners are familiar with and sing it together when David sings it in this story. If you don't have a sung version, simply have children chant the sung response each time it appears.

Listener's guides
FOR GRADES KINDERGARTEN THROUGH 3
- From what kinds of animals did David have to protect his sheep?
- What musical instrument did David play?
- David was a shepherd, a songwriter, a singer, and a soldier, and eventually he became one of the greatest of all: A) sheep farmers B) kings C) house builders.

FOR GRADES 4 THROUGH 8
- Besides being a watchful shepherd, what other talents did Dave show while a child?
- A servant came to the field to tell David to go home, for a great visitor was waiting for him. Who was the visitor?
- Why had this visitor come?
- What effect did David's music have on King Saul?
- Though David was still a boy, what enemy soldier did he face?
- The great King David was able to unite the people of Israel into a _____ _____.

Family and other group discussions
- Have you heard the phrase "from the House of David" read in church? When? (It will be in Scriptures read close to Christmas.)
- David had many talents. Name some of them and how he used them.
- Many of the psalms were written by David. Some are hymns of praise to God and speak of God's greatness, goodness, mercy, power, and justice; others are prayers in times of trouble; still others tell how to be happy in following God. Look at the book of Psalms and find examples of these different kinds of songs.
- In some psalms, David sang of his great trust in God. What does it mean to trust God?

Prayer
Dear Jesus, like David, we sing of your greatness and your love.
(sing) My shepherd is the Lord, nothing indeed shall I want.

Reflections for the storyteller

One of Jesus' most celebrated ancestors was King David. Chosen by God to become king and anointed by the prophet Samuel, David led a remarkable life. His abilities as a warrior and political leader were tremendous. He was a wise and caring king. Often hounded by controversy and heady with power, David made mistakes too, but he looked for God's forgiveness and began again. It is in his music and poetry that the depth of David's soul is revealed to us. In the psalms, we see his struggles and his immeasurable faith in God. While it is uncertain how many he actually wrote, many are attributed to him because he was held in such great esteem. Because of David and other musicians, we too can find God through the poetry of the Old Testament.

The Story

IT BEGAN AS A QUIET DAY. Puffy clouds drifted above while sheep grazed lazily. David, the young shepherd, looked around, but he sensed no danger from wild animals. His sling and stones were always ready, however. More than once he had killed a bear or lion that had come bounding out of the thicket to steal sheep. One shot from David's sling, and the fierce animal lay dead. But today was a quiet day.

The wind rustled the grasses; a few sheep bleated. The young shepherd picked up his harp and began to sing, for David was a poet and musician too. His clear, sweet voice took up a song of his own words. Then David saw a man running toward him. He was a servant of David's father, Jesse, and when he reached David he was almost too breathless to speak. "Your father sends for you," he said, gasping. "Go now."

"Is something wrong?"

"No, but a visitor asks for you. A great man. People in town say he is a seer, a prophet! His name is Samuel. He came to your father's house, saying the Lord had sent him! He said he is to choose the next king from among Jesse's sons!"

David picked up his harp, marveling at these words. The next king? But what of King Saul? Wouldn't he be king for a long time yet?

"Why choose a king from amongst my brothers?" David wondered aloud. "What does he know of us? And if he does choose, it would be Eliab, the eldest. Why must I go?"

"This Samuel says it is not he who chooses, but the Lord. He insists on seeing all of Jesse's sons. Hurry! They're waiting for you!"

Sung Refrain: *My shepherd is the Lord, nothing indeed shall I want.*

David left the field. He was a handsome lad with clear, understanding eyes and a confident walk. Entering his home, he found his entire family and the prophet Samuel waiting for him near the table, which had been set with dinner. His father, Jesse, approached David and said to Samuel, "This is my youngest son, David."

David looked upon Samuel, an old man. Samuel could see in David's eyes the trust David had in God. Closing his own eyes, Samuel remained silent for a moment. Then he opened his eyes and took a horn filled with precious oil from his belt. He walked up to David and anointed him with the special oil. "Someday, you will be a great king, perhaps the greatest king, for God has chosen you," Samuel said.

It was still a quiet day. His family was the same as usual, the house had not changed. But for David, nothing would ever be the same again. He was filled with the spirit of the Lord God, and this spirit would stay with him for the rest of his life. He wore no crown, but now he had been anointed with holy oil, which no one could remove.

    Sung Refrain: *My shepherd is the Lord, nothing indeed shall I want.*

There were many changes ahead for David. The present king, Saul, was a troubled man who no longer trusted in God. Often, he would become so sad and depressed he was unable to go on with his work. His servants suggested that music might help. One said he had heard that a son of Jesse was a skilled harpist whose music was said to soothe many.

    So David was called to the palace, and he spent hours playing his harp and singing his poetry to the king. Saul sat motionless, his eyes downcast. David, his fingers picking out a delicate tune on the harp, sang,

    Sung Refrain: *My shepherd is the Lord, nothing indeed shall I want.*

The king looked up, much soothed. Soon the servants said that David the musician was a healer too. David next discovered the warrior in himself. King Saul's army, in which some of David's brothers were soldiers, was fighting the Philistines. One day, David took food to his brothers. There he saw a frightening scene: in the Philistine army was a huge man, a giant of a man named Goliath, who taunted the Israelites every morning and every night.

    David saw that Goliath was enormous. He was much taller than the tallest man of the Israelites. His shoulders were broader than any others, his arms and legs were like tree trunks. His massive armor glinted in the sun, and he roared at Saul's men, "Why must we fight a war? Let one man come forward to fight me! If he kills me, we will be your slaves. If I kill your soldier, you will be our slaves!" And then he laughed a terrible laugh.

    David, still a boy, took out his sling. Had he not killed lions? Had he not killed bears? Would God not protect him as he slew this bear of a man? The boy approached the giant.

    Goliath laughed again. "Am I a dog that you come to me with sticks?"

    But David, with five smooth stones in his pouch, ran toward the towering enemy. As if a lion were about to devour his sheep, David fitted a stone into his sling. It whizzed through the air and hit Goliath in the forehead. The huge man crumbled to the ground, dead.

    After that, David became part of the army, and soon the soldiers said that David was a good warrior.

    Sung Refrain: *My shepherd is the Lord, nothing indeed shall I want.*

David continued to sing for the king, and then he began his life as a leader of soldiers. Someday he would become a celebrated warrior, and he would write and sing more songs. Then, he would become the exalted King David. King David would unite the people of Israel into a great nation. During his reign, he would do what he thought was right, but sometimes he would make mistakes. Always he would trust in God. He would ask for forgiveness, and he would ask for guidance. Yes, he would become a king who would be remembered for all time, but he would also remain a faithful servant of God.

    Sung Refrain: *My shepherd is the Lord, nothing indeed shall I want.*

SHORTER VERSION

David was the youngest in a family of eight boys. He was a very talented child and God had big plans for him.

David was a shepherd of his father's sheep. In the quiet fields, he often thought of God and sang songs to God. Sometimes, though, a bear or lion tried to take one of the sheep. Then David put a stone into his sling shot. He was so good, he'd hit the big animal in one try and save the sheep.

Once David was sent to take food to his brothers who were soldiers. There he learned that the army they were fighting had a huge soldier named Goliath, a giant of man. Everyone was very afraid of Goliath. Not David. He grabbed his sling shot. Just as a hungry lion would come running at the sheep, Goliath came at David. Zing! went the stone from David's slingshot. And down went Goliath! Little David had saved his brothers and other soldiers! When David grew up, he became a great leader in the army.

But David wasn't just a shepherd with a good aim who became a soldier. He was also a musician. He wrote many songs, which he sang as he played his harp. David was asked to come to King Saul's palace. Saul was unhappy, for he no longer loved God. David's songs were about God's love. He sang them to the king, who then felt better.

But David wasn't just a singer-songwriter-shepherd-soldier! Samuel the prophet had blessed David, because God wanted David to be the next king. David became one of the greatest kings of all time.

The story of Solomon
Based on 1 Kings 3:4-28; 5:9; 6; 7; 10:1-13

Why is this person on the Jesse Tree?
- Solomon was the son of King David, Jesus' most well-known ancestor.
- He is remembered for his tremendous wisdom.

Listener's guides
FOR GRADES KINDERGARTEN THROUGH 3
- Who is the woman who went to visit King Solomon?
- How many songs did King Solomon write? A) 24 B) less than 100 C) more than 1000.
- When King Solomon prayed, he asked God for an understanding _____.

FOR GRADES 4 THROUGH 8
- Why did the Queen of Sheba want to meet King Solomon?
- Of his wealth, songwriting, and wisdom, which is Solomon best remembered for?
- What did God ask Solomon in a dream?
- What was Solomon's answer?
- Name two of Solomon's interests.
- The Queen of Sheba had many gifts for King Solomon, but she also had many _____.

Family and other group discussions
- Two mothers consulted with King Solomon. Do you think King Solomon actually intended to have the baby killed, or was he "calling their bluff"?
- Discuss one of Solomon's sayings.
- What were some of Solomon's interests and talents?
- When Solomon first became king, he felt he lacked leadership skills. Discuss specifically what he asked of God. What kinds of skills do you think leaders of today need? Which of these would follow Jesus' teachings?

Prayer
Dear God, thank you for the example of the good King Solomon. May we too learn fairness, caring, and openness. Amen.

Reflections for the storyteller
Jesus was born a child of poverty and powerlessness, but, centuries before his birth, his ancestor King Solomon possessed vast wealth and power. Solomon, David's son, reigned in a time of peace, and he was able to construct the magnificent temple that David had hoped to build. But for all this, Solomon is most revered for his wisdom and understanding heart. Solomon's story is a story of God's blessings, for everything that he is remembered for were gifts from God.

The Story

BECAUSE SHE WAS QUEEN, SHE HAD MET MANY POWERFUL PEOPLE. She had known many who were wealthy, like she was. Because of her position, she had sought out those who were wise, too. But it was the stories of King Solomon of Israel that most intrigued her. Some said he was more powerful than other kings. Others said he was the wealthiest king to ever live. Still others talked of his incredible wisdom. She, the queen of Sheba of Arabia, wanted to meet this man. She was on her way there now.

The queen was very aware that she held a position of great honor, too. Hers was not a time when women normally held power. Even those born into royal families had little to say of their own futures, much less the futures of their countries. But she was the queen, the one who ruled, the one who must be wise. Now she sought out the man whose wisdom had become legendary. His wealth and power interested her, but it was his wisdom that she most wanted to witness. She kept thinking of the stories she had heard, and one in particular haunted her.

Two women came to Solomon, the story tells, with a newborn baby. Each claimed the child was hers.

"We each had newborn sons, my Lord," the first woman explained. "In the night, hers died. She woke, saw her baby was dead, and took my living child. She put the dead baby next to me as I slept. In the morning, I awoke and saw the baby was dead, and then realized he wasn't my baby. This child is mine!"

"She lies!" the second woman insisted. "The live child is mine!"

"No, no! He's my child!" the first persisted.

They continued to argue before the king.

King Solomon listened. Then he said, "Bring me a sword."

A silence fell upon the room as a sword was brought. "Cut the living child in two and give half to each woman," the king calmly said.

"My Lord, please do not harm the child! Give him to her, but please, do not kill the baby!" cried the first woman.

"He shall belong to neither of us," the second woman said. "Divide him."

Then King Solomon spoke, "Give the child to the first woman. Do not kill him. She is his mother."

The Queen of Sheba thought of this story as she traveled closer to Israel. It was said that Solomon had a heart as vast as the sand on the seashore. That was a man she wanted to meet. She heard, too, that Solomon had written more than a thousand songs. He could speak knowledgeably of trees and plant life. He knew much about birds, reptiles, fish, and other animals. And his wise sayings particularly fascinated her:

"Better a dinner of vegetables where love is than a fatted ox and hatred with it."

"The mouths of fools are their ruin, and their lips a snare to themselves."

"When you make a vow to God, do not delay fulfilling it; for God has no pleasure in fools. Fulfill what you vow."

The Queen now wondered about King Solomon's God. She had heard that all this wisdom, power, and wealth were bestowed upon Solomon by God. Long ago, when he had just become king, he had been visited by his God in a dream. God had asked the young Solomon what he wanted.

"God, my God, I am unskilled in leadership, yet you have made me king of this people of yours, a people so vast they cannot be counted. Please give me, your servant, an understanding heart, so I can decide between good and evil," Solomon had answered.

God had been pleased. "Since you have asked for this and not for riches or a long life, I will give you a heart wise and shrewd as none before you has had and none will have after you. I will also give you what you have not asked for: you will have riches greater than any other king, and a long life."

Solomon then awoke and praised God, offering thanksgiving.

The queen had heard that all that the dream had predicted had come true. Now, she traveled to see for herself.

She did not come empty-handed. She and her servants traveled with camels loaded with costly spices, great quantities of gold, and precious stones. She was bringing King Solomon gifts, but she came to question him.

The queen of Sheba arrived in Jerusalem. She admired the temple that Solomon had built, the temple where he worshiped. It was constructed with the finest of wood, the best of stone. Fragrant cedar wood was carved into roses, olive wood angel statues looked upon worshipers, and gold covered the inside of the temple. A golden altar and table were some of the furnishings.

In the streets the queen saw a thousand chariots and thousands of horses. She saw ivory, gold, jewels, armor, spices, and exquisite fabrics all around her. She saw the fleet of ships he owned. Then she saw the palace, with its ornate bronze pillars, filled with well-dressed, well-fed servants. The Queen of Sheba was stunned. Even she had never seen so much wealth.

She went to Solomon, arrayed in her own glory and wealth. He received her graciously, as he did all the royal visitors who brought him gifts. The Queen of Sheba would give him her gifts, but first, there was something more important.

The queen began questioning the king. She asked question after question, one more difficult than the next. And King Solomon answered them, one by one, carefully, correctly, wisely. Finally, her questions stopped.

She said, "What I heard about you in my own country was true! Until I came and saw it with my own eyes, I could not believe what they told me, yet they told me less than half. For wisdom and prosperity you surpass the report I heard. How happy your family and servants must be! I know it is because of your God that you possess so much, in all ways. Blessed be God, your God who has granted you his favor! Because of your God's love for this people, you are able to deal with law and justice."

Then she gave him one hundred and twenty talents of gold, precious stones, and a wealth of spices, more than was ever given to King Solomon. He in turn gave her many gifts from his bounty. And she returned home.

SHORTER VERSION

Solomon had grown up watching his father, King David, at work. Now Solomon was king and he didn't feel ready for this big job.

Like his father, Solomon knew that God loved and cared for him. One night, God came to Solomon in a dream, asking the young king what he wanted. "God, my God," said Solomon, "you have made me king of so many people they cannot be counted! Please give me an understanding heart. Then I will be able to make good decisions and become a caring king."

This made God happy. "Since you have asked for this, and not for riches, I will make you so wise you will always be known for your wisdom. But I will also give you what you didn't ask for: you will have riches greater than any other king."

All this happened. In Solomon's kingdom, there were thousands of chariots and as many horses. There were beautiful and costly things like jewels, spices, ivory, and gold. Solomon had many servants, all well-fed and well-dressed. And Solomon had a temple built with the finest woods. There he prayed, amongst the fragrant wood that had been carved into roses and angels, near an altar made of gold.

After hundreds and hundreds of years, it is not for his things that we remember King Solomon, however. For Solomon was such a caring and wise king, he is remembered today as the wisest king of all.

The story of Elijah

Based on 1 Kings 17:1-24; 18:20-46; 2 Kings 2:1-13

Why is this person on the Jesse Tree?
- Elijah, one of the greatest prophets of the Hebrew Scriptures, is fourth in line of people mentioned in those Scriptures, after Abraham, Moses and David.
- In the Transfiguration (Matthew 17:1-13), Elijah appeared with Moses beside Jesus.
- Jesus himself refers to Elijah as a forerunner of John the Baptist.

Reading this story
Tell listeners that there is a Jewish custom at the Seder meal at Passover of leaving the door ajar and setting a place at the table for Elijah. Encourage them to listen for the reason for this tradition.

Listener's guides
FOR GRADES KINDERGARTEN THROUGH 3
- What was Elijah wearing when the woman first saw him?
- What kind of bird brought food to Elijah?
- A special chariot and horses came for Elijah. What were they made of?

FOR GRADES 4 THROUGH 8
- Describe Elijah's appearance.
- Name two ways Elijah saved the woman's son.
- How did Elijah get food before he came to the family's house?
- What was the challenge Elijah made to followers of the false god Baal?
- What was the weather condition at the time of this story?
- How did Elijah leave?

Family and other group discussions
- Elijah is considered one of the most powerful and interesting people in the Hebrew Scriptures. Find examples in the story of what he did to earn himself this reputation. Further this discussion by reading accounts of Elijah in 1 Kings, chapters 17 and 18, and 2 Kings, chapter 2.
- Elijah is mentioned several times in the Christian Scriptures, including Matthew 17:1–13, Mark 8:28, Luke 1:17 and 9:18–21.
- Are there prophets today?

Prayer
Dear God, sometimes a person needs to be strong and do hard things to do your work in the world. Help us to appreciate Elijah's courage and to find our own courage when needed. Amen.

Reflections for the storyteller
The great prophet Elijah ministered during the years 874–852 B.C. He came from the desert highlands of Gilead during a time when Israel's leaders were choosing false gods over the true God. But Elijah was not going to sit idly by as his country turned away from God. He performed miracles and preached, predicting the downfall of Israel. Elijah was so influential that he is mentioned many times in the New Testament in relation to Jesus. During Christ's public years, some people thought him to be Elijah, who was expected to return. In the

Transfiguration, it was Elijah, along with Moses, who appeared with Jesus. But it was John the Baptist whom Jesus connected to Elijah.

The Story

SO THAT IS WHAT HAPPENED TO THE HOLY MAN, the widow in Zarephath thought after she had heard the news. She sat quietly and reflected on all that had occurred. Astounding as this news was, it did not surprise her. Somehow, it was right.

Her son, now a strong boy in his teens, came in.

"Do you remember Elijah?" she asked.

"How can I ever forget him? He saved my life!" was her son's response.

"He did not just save it—he got it back for you," she said.

"He saved me twice. Do you remember how we were starving before he came?" the boy said. "We had no more food and you thought we would soon die."

She nodded, more at the memory than at her son. "I was desperate. The drought had gone on so long, and I had no way of feeding you. I was gathering sticks for one last fire to make the last bread before we died. And when I looked up, there stood Elijah. He wore a goatskin cloak, and his hair was long. He asked me to bring him some water, and as I turned to do so, he called after me, asking for some bread. I could tell he was an Israelite, so I answered, 'As the Lord your God lives, I have no baked bread, only a handful of meal and a bit of oil left. My son and I will soon die.' I will never forget what he replied."

The son remained silent, waiting for his mother's memories.

"'Do not be afraid. Go and make some bread for yourself and your son and for me also. For the God of Israel says, "Jar of meal shall not be spent, jug of oil shall not be emptied, before the day when God sends rain on the face of the earth."' And we never ran out of food!"

Her son nodded. "Because of him, we had food—he saved me then. He stayed with us for quite a while. I asked him how he had eaten before he came to us, and he said the ravens brought him food—bread every morning, meat every night! I loved hearing that, but at the time I didn't believe him."

"Oh, I have no doubt that what he said was true. What is that compared to raising you back to life?"

A faraway look came over the son's face.

The mother spoke, "I will never, never forget that day. You fell ill. I was terrified that I would lose you, too, as I had lost your father, but I could not save you. Elijah came in just as you had died. I was holding you and weeping. Elijah took you into his arms, took your body up to the upper room, and laid you down on the bed. I heard his loud voice calling, 'Yahweh my God, may the breath of life, I beg you, come into this child again!' Though I was filled with grief and despair, those words, that voice, seemed to go right through me."

Her son remembered, "I sat up then, I remember, and he took me back downstairs to you. I didn't understand what happened."

There were tears in the mother's eyes now. "You were alive! I can still see him, climbing down, and you—alive! awake!—in his arms! At that moment, I truly knew that Elijah was a man of God."

"When he left here, he proved that to many others, too. He fought so hard against the king and queen's belief in the false god, Baal. Oh, how I wish I had been there when he challenged the prophets of Baal to sacrifice a bull to Baal, and have Baal himself light the fire!"

She laughed. "I heard they prayed and cried and begged all morning and all afternoon, but their god never responded."

"But Elijah waited patiently, and then he repaired the altar to God, putting twelve stones around it for the twelve sons of Jacob. Then he poured water—precious water in that drought!—all over the altar and wood, so it would be impossible to light. Then Elijah prayed—-"

"He was a prayerful man, and it was thrilling to hear him call upon God!" the mother exclaimed.

"Elijah asked God to send a fire, so the people there would again believe in the Lord, and not in false gods. And the fire rained down, burning that soaked wood. Then the people fell to the ground, in awe of the true God. Later, Elijah killed all the prophets of Baal. And the drought ended then, too, because God wanted it to."

"But Mother, what made you think of him today? Has something happened?"

She nodded. "I have heard that Elijah is gone…"

"He died?"

She smiled. "Well no, but I heard he has chosen a successor, a man named Elisha. They traveled to Bethel, then to Jericho, then on to the river Jordan. When they reached the river, Elijah struck the waters with his cloak…"

"That cloak!" the son said, amused.

"And the waters divided, just as they did for Moses! The two crossed, and Elisha told others later that a chariot appeared—just appeared. It was made of fire, pulled by horses also made of fire! It came nearer until it stood between them. Then, Elijah was taken up to heaven in a whirlwind!"

The mother finished her story, and both remained silent, awed.

Then she stood up, looking up toward the room where Elijah had once slept, and had once brought her son back to life.

"He truly was a man of God," she said quietly, reverently.

Her son stood beside her. "He will be back," he said. "Elijah will return."

SHORTER VERSION

The woman already knew that Elijah was a man of God. She had seen a miracle the very first day he arrived at her home.

There had been three years of drought. With no rain, there was no food, and people were starving. The woman and her young son were about to die when Elijah came. He told her that God would not let them die of hunger. From that time on, until the drought was over, she always had enough flour and oil to make bread.

Still she did not expect he could save her child a second time! When the boy became sick and died quickly, Elijah came in to see the mother weeping. In a loud voice, he prayed over the child's body, begging God to bring life back to the child. And the little boy sat up!

So, years later, perhaps the woman was not so surprised when she heard what happened to the holy man, Elijah: a chariot, made of fire, pulled by horses also made of fire, came and took Elijah to God. Elijah never died!

And to this day, people wait for the return of Elijah.

The story of Isaiah

Based on Isaiah 6:1–13; 9:1, 5–6

Why is this person on the Jesse Tree?
- Isaiah, a great prophet, foretold the coming of Jesus. His writings form the longest book in Scripture.
- His writings are frequent readings during Advent.

Reading this story
The words of the seraphim are presented here as a refrain if you choose to have listener participation.

Listener's guides
FOR GRADES KINDERGARTEN THROUGH 3
- Who did Isaiah work for?
- A seraph is a kind of _____.
- Circle the correct answer: God and angels came to Isaiah in a 1) bus 2) lake 3) vision.

FOR GRADES 4 THROUGH 8
- Name some of Isaiah's skills that helped the king.
- Describe a seraph.
- Why did Isaiah cry out?
- In a vision, Isaiah became cleansed when a seraph touched his lips with a _____.
- What was Isaiah's greatest prophesy?
- Isaiah predicted that Jesus would be called the _____ of Peace.

Family and other group discussions and Prayer
- Read Isaiah 7:14; 9:2, 6; 35:5–6; 40:1–5, 9, 11; 60:1–3. George Frideric Handel used these scriptures and others in composing *Messiah*. Listen to the most famous part of this piece, the *Hallelujah Chorus*.

Reflections for the storyteller
The kingdom of Israel, once so strong under the leadership of King David, broke up in the years after the death of Solomon. Ten of the tribes, called Israel, went north, and made Shechem their capital. The remaining two, Judah and Benjamin, united and became known as the tribe of Judah, whose capital was Jerusalem. Internal strife set in and worshiping false gods continued (as in the story of Elijah).

A nation called Assyria rose swiftly to power and overran the ten tribes. They scattered the vanquished Israelites so they could not reunite. That is the last of what is known of those ten tribes.

Many years later, the Babylonians captured Judah, claiming the Holy Land and destroying the city of Jerusalem. The conquered tribe of Judah was led into captivity in Babylon, where their name was changed to Jews, from the Hebrew word "Yehudi," meaning "belonging to the tribe of Judah." It was prior to this exile in Babylon that Elijah worked, and another voice was heard at this time: that of Isaiah. Isaiah, a statesman who worked with the king, warned and predicted this downfall of Judah, but his warning fell on deaf ears. After the capture and exile to Babylon, Isaiah's followers continued to prophesy. It was through Isaiah that the coming of Jesus was foretold.

The Story

ISAIAH WAS A WELL-EDUCATED MAN WHO OFTEN WORKED FOR THE KING. He had a gift for recognizing the ways that governments worked. He understood how wars started, and he wanted to avoid them. Frequently the king called upon him for advice.

But Isaiah loved and believed in a much higher king. He was a follower of God. One day, he was called upon by God through a vision!

He saw the Lord sitting on a throne, high and lofty. The hem of God's robe filled the temple! Attending God were seraphim, a kind of angel. Each seraph had six wings: with two they covered their faces, and with two they covered their feet, and with two they flew. The seraphim called to one another:

> **Refrain** *Holy, holy, holy is the Lord! God's glory fills the whole earth!*

Isaiah felt the foundations of the doorways shake as they cried out, and the temple was filled with smoke. He cried, "How unhappy I am! I am lost, for I am a man of unclean, sinful lips, and I live among a sinful people, a people of unclean lips. Yet, my eyes have looked at the King, the Lord!"

One of the seraphim flew to him, holding a live coal taken from the altar with a pair of tongs. The seraph touched Isaiah's lips with the coal and said, "Now that this has touched your lips, you are cleansed, your guilt has departed, and your sin is blotted out."

Then Isaiah heard the voice of God saying, "Whom shall I send? Who will be our messenger?"

And Isaiah answered, "Here I am. Send me!"

> **Refrain:** *Holy, holy, holy is the Lord! God's glory fills the whole earth!*

So, Isaiah became a great prophet, the voice of God. He advised the king and the people. He prophesied the coming destruction of their country; he scolded people for living badly. His words were filled with wisdom and hope for God's great love. The people of his time did not listen, but later people would read the words of Isaiah and take them to heart.

It was Isaiah's voice that foretold the greatest event: the coming of the Messiah, the Savior who would be Jesus.

Isaiah was on the far side of the Jordan River when he prophesied:

"The people that walked in darkness have seen a great light; on those who live in a land of deep shadow a light has shone.

"For there is a child born for us, a son given us, and dominion is laid on his shoulders, and this is the name they give him: Wonder Counselor, Mighty God, Eternal Father, Prince of Peace."

> **Refrain:** *Holy, holy, holy is the Lord! God's glory fills the whole earth!*

The story of Nehemiah

Based on Nehemiah 1; 2; 3; 4; 7:1; 12:27-43

Why is this person on the Jesse Tree?
- A few hundred years before Jesus' birth, Nehemiah rebuilt part of Jerusalem and restored the integrity of the Jewish people, who had been in exile in Babylon.

Reading this story
This story lends itself to some rousing participation with younger children. Choose listeners to be in either the Nehemiah chorus or Sanballat chorus. End the story with the two groups as the celebratory choirs. They can march separately around the sides of the room and meet in the center for a song of praise and thanksgiving.

Listener's guides
FOR GRADES KINDERGARTEN THROUGH 3
- What did the king notice about Nehemiah?
- Choose the correct answer: Sanballat and others A) brought pizza to Nehemiah B) came to make fun of Nehemiah and the other workers C) offered to help build the wall.
- Where did the people march to celebrate finishing the wall?

FOR GRADES 4 THROUGH 8
- Nehemiah was living in _____ before returning to Jerusalem.
- What was wrong in Jerusalem?
- Who was against Nehemiah's plan to rebuild?
- How did Nehemiah plan to rebuild such a large wall?
- Why must Nehemiah call for some of the workers to stand guard instead?
- How long did it take to rebuild the wall?

Family and other group discussions
- Nehemiah and some others were forced to live for years in Babylon, far from their culture. Nehemiah remained faithful to his religious beliefs. Discuss why this would be very difficult. Is this difficult for us?
- Nehemiah understood those living in Jerusalem had come to feel disheartened about their lives as well as their city. He managed to rebuild not only the wall but also the people's pride and self-worth. How did building a wall help them emotionally? Do we feel a pride and a sense of self-worth within our community?

Prayer
Please help us, Lord, to face our challenges. And give us compassionate hearts and alert minds to see when others need us to help with their challenges. Amen.

Reflections for the storyteller
The Jews' time of exile in Babylon was unlike their ancestors' enslavement in Egypt of Moses' time. In Babylon, they were assimilated into Babylonian culture, so there was great danger of losing their identity as Jews, of losing sight of the true God, and lapsing into the comfortable ways of the Babylonians.

Then, Persia defeated the Babylonians. King

Cyrus of Persia permitted the Jews to leave Babylon and return to Jerusalem and the surrounding land. The Jews went back in waves, nothing like the frantic exodus out of Egypt. Back in the Promised Land, they faced both a devastated city and a damaged identity. It was under these conditions that Nehemiah began his work.

Nehemiah reconstructed the wall surrounding Jerusalem, and he rebuilt the integrity of the Jews by drawing on the strength and abilities of the community. In Scripture, Nehemiah told his own story. He will do so here, too.

The Story

I AM NEHEMIAH, SON OF HACALIAH. I was living in Babylon, working for King Artaxerxes. He was a kind man, and I was on very good terms with him.

I was also a devout Jew, living far away from the holy city of Jerusalem. Often I heard about my fellow Jews who had recently returned to Jerusalem after our many years of exile in Babylon. My friend Hanani told me, "They are in great trouble. The protective walls surrounding Jerusalem are in ruins and the gates burned down. Over the years, armies have swept through leaving rubble everywhere. In fact, the people are using these remains to rebuild their houses! They went back to Jerusalem with such high hopes. But they are in despair now."

I wept. I cried out to my God to help me help my people. My sadness was so great the king asked me if I was ill. Respectfully I told him of the despair of my people. That good king asked me what I wanted. Silently I prayed. Then I said aloud, "If it pleases the king, I ask for leave to go to the land of my ancestors, to help rebuild it."

The king not only gave me permission to leave for an extended time, but he also gave me letters granting me the authority to govern when I got there, as well as lumber to help with the building!

Traveling toward my homeland, I showed my papers to other leaders along the way so they would let me pass through their lands. When the governor of nearby Samaria, Sanballat by name, heard of my power and of my mission, he was very angry. He did not want anyone to help the children of Israel. He would make trouble for me.

Sanballat Chorus: *Nehemiah, go back to Babylon. Leave Jerusalem alone!*

When I reached Jerusalem, I kept to myself at first. I set up camp and at night, made my way around the ruined wall, inspecting and planning. The devastation was bad. Repair work would be enormous. But I did not despair, for God was with us. For three nights I made my rounds unseen, silently planning.

Then I called a meeting. Everyone came: the high priest, the goldsmiths, the perfumers, the homeowners. To this crowd I spoke, "You see the trouble we are in: Jerusalem is in ruins, and there is no protective wall. Even the gates have been burned. But we can rebuild the walls. Let's give ourselves protection once again. Let's give Jerusalem the dignity this great city deserves!"

Then I told them that I believed that God's favor was upon us, and the king supports us. They listened, but they knew the task ahead was an overwhelming one. So I went on, "This job is too big for any one group. It will take all of us working together to complete it. I'll organize small groups, and each will take a section. Work hard on your section and make it sound. Put your pride into it, for your work will contribute to the whole. Your section will make our city strong once again."

Their response was great.

> **Nehemiah Chorus:** *"Let's build! Let's begin! We will be strong once again!"*

They began immediately, bringing tools, getting lumber. I organized work crews, choosing who truly believed in our project and our city. Anyone could work, their skills did not matter. I traveled about, seeing that each section was being repaired, making certain there were enough workers in each place.

Eliashib, the high priest, and the other priests rebuilt the Sheep Gate. Uzziel of the goldsmiths' guild worked next to Hananiah of the perfumers' guild. Rephaiah, ruler of half a district of Jerusalem, came to work. Some people carried out repairs in front of their own houses.

Of course, Sanballat came, bringing others to ridicule us. They found me as I worked with Hananiah. They called to us, sneers on their faces.

> **Sanballat Chorus:** *"What are you doing? Are you planning to revolt against the king?"*

Then they laughed mockingly at us. Hananiah and his workers silently kept at their tasks, but I called back calmly, "The God of heaven will give us success. We, God's servants, are going to build!"

And we did. Little by little, the wall was being rebuilt. And, little by little, the good Jewish folk working were feeling better and better. They said,

> **Nehemiah Chorus:** *"There's hope! Our city will be strong again. We will succeed!"*

Sanballat went into a rage when he heard this. He came by again to jeer at us, saying,

> **Sanballat Chorus:** *"What are you pathetic people trying to do? Do you expect to finish in one day? Do you think you can put new life into these charred stones?"*

Soon he began to plot. I learned he was gathering a group to attack us. Quickly, I called a meeting. "God is with us," I reminded the workers. "We'll set up a watch, day and night."

Some exclaimed,

> **Nehemiah Chorus:** *"There's still so much to do! And now there are threats to our safety! We will never finish!"*

That was followed by murmurs that became shouts of agreement. They were losing heart and fear was taking over, just as Sanballat hoped.

I said, "Don't be afraid. Keep your minds on the Lord! Each family must post guards, armed with swords, spears, and bows. We will not let them stop us!"

That is what happened. We organized, and our enemies, learning that God had thwarted their plan, withdrew.

The work went on, with hope and pride renewed. But from then on, only half the people worked. The others stood guard. I had a trumpeter ready to sound an alarm if needed.

We worked from the break of day until the stars appeared. Night and day we always kept watch. In only fifty-two days the wall was completed, for the hearts of the people were in their work, and God was with us.

Of course, we held a ceremony to dedicate the wall. The people of Jerusalem joined into two choirs and marched along the top of the wall, one to the right, the other to the left. They played trumpets, harps, cymbals, and lutes, coming together at the temple. The music carried us joyfully for hours. The jubilation of Jerusalem was heard for miles around.

SHORTER VERSION

MY NAME IS NEHEMIAH AND I HAD A HUGE JOB TO DO. See the wall that used to surround the holy city of Jerusalem? It was broken and crumbling in many places. The gates were burned. Whole chunks of the wall were gone.

I love this city and the people who are trying to live in it. After years of being forced to live in Babylon, we are slowly returning home. Once again, we can live as Jews. We can live in the ways that are important to us.

However, when I came back, I could see that the people were unhappy. They didn't believe things could get better.

This was understandable, for the work of rebuilding the city was staggering. But I knew absolutely that God was with us! And I knew that if we did it right, building the wall would also "rebuild" the people. They could become strong and happy once more.

I organized teams. Each team would build just one section of the wall, but it would be a section that they would feel proud of when they finished. These people were not builders but they had each other to learn from and to share the burden.

Others came from a nearby area to make fun of us. They shouted and even threatened to attack us. But God was with us. We finished the whole wall in just fifty-two days! Then we had a grand celebration! We celebrated because the city was once again protected and we had been the ones to do this. But there was additional happiness because we were now getting our beloved Jerusalem back again.

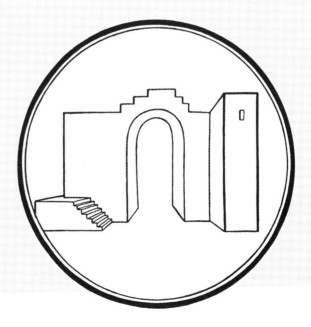

The story of Jonah
Based on the book of Jonah

Why is this person on the Jesse Tree?
- While we don't know if Jonah's story is fact or fiction, it is important because it has themes that are part of Christ's teachings. It is about people's ability to hurt each other, and their ability to overcome evil, and above all, God's forgiveness and love.

Reading this story
Because this is a lengthy story, consider having two readers.

Listener's guides
FOR GRADES KINDERGARTEN THROUGH 3
- What was Nineveh?
- What was the weather like when Jonah was on the ship?
- How did Jonah get back to land?

FOR GRADES 4 THROUGH 8
- What frightened Jonah about going to Nineveh?
- Instead of going to Nineveh, where did Jonah go?
- What were Jonah's first thoughts when he was swallowed by the huge fish?
- Were Jonah's fears about the people of Nineveh correct?
- What did the king of Nineveh propose?
- What are Jonah's mood and thoughts at the end of the story?

Family and Other Group Discussions
- Jonah's prayers change in tone over the course of the story. Talk about ways of praying. Do you ever pray when you are angry?
- Does this story end in a typical way? How does the ending make you feel?
- What do you think the writer of this story is telling us?
- God is patient with both Jonah and the people of Nineveh. Consider God's patience with us.

Prayer
Like Jonah, we are not perfect. We are human, and so we make mistakes. We get angry and frustrated. God, you who made us human, thank you for being patient with us! Amen.

Reflections for the storyteller
The prophet Jonah ben Amittai was a historical figure who lived about two hundred years after the renowned kings David and Solomon. There is great debate about this story. The author was not Jonah himself, but used Jonah's revered name to give credit to his story. Some say it is reliable history, while others say it is a wonderful parable. Christians may see Jonah as prefiguring Christ, for as Jesus says in Matthew's gospel, just as Jonah spent three days in the belly of the fish so will "the Son of Man" spend three days in the heart of the earth. Moslems call Jonah "Yunus," and some claim there is a mosque that holds his tomb and

a tooth from the fish that swallowed him. The Jews read his story each year in observance of the sacred Day of Atonement, because it is a story of God's great mercy and compassion for those who seek repentance and forgiveness.

The book of Jonah leaves us with a challenge. It ends with a question posed by God to Jonah. We don't learn of Jonah's answer. Perhaps that is so the readers of each generation will seek to answer it for themselves.

The Story

Reader One: Jonah was a prophet. It was not an easy job, and some days were harder than others. But this—this was the worst day of all!

Yahweh told Jonah to preach to the people of Nineveh—Nineveh! Jonah had heard about that great city: it was so large that the wall surrounding it was eight miles long and one hundred feet high! And inside that wall was a city so vast and so rich there were fifteen hundred towers on buildings and temples to many gods. Water was brought in from thirty miles away!

The real issue was that the citizens were unbelievers, not followers of God. And he, Jonah, was to travel to Nineveh and tell those pagan people that God was unhappy with them? If anyone at all listened to him, they would laugh him out of town—or throw him out.

Reader Two: Jonah set his chin stubbornly. God must plan to be merciful to the citizens of Nineveh, those wicked people. Why should he, Jonah, help them? They didn't deserve to be saved! Besides, it was over five hundred miles to Nineveh…

No, he wasn't going to do it. Jonah fled in the opposite direction, to the seaport town of Joppa. There he boarded a ship bound for Tarshish, a place so far away it was called "the end of the world." Oh, what a relief! He'd never get to Nineveh now. Jonah was so relaxed he went down into the hold and fell asleep.

Reader One: While Jonah was sleeping, God sent a great wind upon the sea. As the storm raged, the sailors feared the ship would be destroyed and they would all drown. Throwing cargo overboard to lighten their load, the sailors all cried out to their various gods, begging to be saved. When they found Jonah was asleep, they shouted to him to pray to his God. Then they decided if they cast lots, the one who lost was the one who was causing the storm. Jonah lost.

Desperately, one sailor asked him, "What is your business? Where do you come from?"

"I am Hebrew. I worship the Lord God of heaven and earth," Jonah answered. "I am causing the storm, I'm sure. Throw me overboard, and the sea will grow calm. I don't want you to suffer because of me."

Reader Two: The sailors didn't really want to do this. Instead, they rowed hard, trying to reach shore, but the storm only grew worse. Finally, they prayed to Jonah's God, saying they were doing what they thought God wanted. Then they threw Jonah overboard. Immediately, the waters grew calm, and the sailors trembled in a new kind of fear.

Reader One: Jonah plunged down, down, down into the sea. This was it. The end. He should have gone to Nineveh. But suddenly a dark shadow passed in front of him, and in the murky waters he realized it was the huge, open jaws of a great fish. God had arranged that the fish swallow him. Before Jonah could struggle, he was in the belly of the fish!

At first Jonah was relieved. Here he could breathe! He would not drown. Then he looked around. Seaweed, small fish, and bones floated around him. Bones. How long would it be before those bones included his? It was dark and it smelled. Would he starve first, or be digested?

Reader Two: Water surrounded him up to his throat and seaweed wrapped around his head. And Jonah despaired. He cried out to God. He was deeply sorry for not having gone to Nineveh. Would God please forgive him and give him another chance? For three days and three nights, Jonah waited and prayed in the belly of the fish.

Reader One: God spoke to the fish, and the fish spat Jonah onto the shore. He landed on the sand. He blinked in the daylight. He breathed the fresh air in deeply. He untangled the seaweed from his fingers and hair. Jonah shivered until he began feeling the warm sunlight on his skin. It was so good to be alive!

Then he heard God's voice. "Up, Jonah. Go to Nineveh. Preach to the people there as I have told you."

Reader Two: This time there was no argument from Jonah. He arrived at the wicked, beautiful city several days later. Jonah saw its richness and sighed with despair. What was the point? Why would anyone here believe him? Even if some did, Jonah thought bitterly, they did not deserve God's love. Still, he had to try. He dragged himself around all day, talking to people alone or standing on steps and preaching. "Only forty more days and Nineveh will be destroyed!" he shouted.

Reader One: Much to Jonah's amazement, the people listened. They told Jonah that they would fast and wear sackcloth (rough clothing), to show that they were sorry. News of this reached the king. He rose from his throne, took off his royal robes, and dressed in sackcloth. He proclaimed, "People and all animals are to eat nothing or drink water for three days. All must call upon God, saying we will change our evil ways!"

And the citizens of Nineveh fasted and prayed. God heard their prayers and had mercy on them. No disaster destroyed their city.

Reader Two: Now Jonah was furious. His prayers were angry ones. "Isn't this what I said would happen when I was still at home? That's why I fled to Tarshish. I knew you were a God of tenderness and compassion. I knew you would be slow to anger, that you would relent!" Jonah was so disgusted, he added, "So now, God, please take my life away."

Reader One: God said simply, "Are you right to be this angry?" Jonah stomped off, going east of the city. Some distance away, so he could see the city, Jonah made himself a shelter. He was still angry. God provided a vine to soothe him. It grew up over Jonah's shelter, and Jonah delighted in it. At dawn, God sent a worm to attack the vine, so it withered. When the sun had risen, God sent a scorching wind. Jonah was so overcome with heat and misery, he called out to God, again begging for death.

Reader Two: God asked, "Are you right to be so angry about the plant?"

Jonah muttered, "I have every right to be angry, to the point of death!"

"You feel pity for the vine, which you did not plant or tend. It lived only one day. So should I not feel pity for Nineveh, for the one hundred and twenty thousand people who do not know right from wrong, to say nothing of the animals?"

Jonah was silent. For once he did not know how to answer.

SHORTER VERSION

JONAH WAS A PROPHET. His job was to listen to God and then tell people what God said.

One day, Jonah was in a very bad mood. God said, "Go to Nineveh. Tell the people there I am unhappy with how they are living."

No way, thought Jonah. I am not traveling five hundred miles to tell some people who hardly know God that God wants them to change their ways! They will throw me out of town! Quickly, Jonah boarded a ship which was going even further away from Nineveh than Jonah was already.

God didn't give up easily. A storm broke and soon the ship was being tossed about in great waves. Jonah ended up in the water. But that wasn't the end. He ended up being swallowed by a huge fish!

There he was, sitting in the belly of the fish. What do you think he saw there? What might it have smelled like? Was it dark or could he see? Whatever his experience, Jonah wanted out! He prayed, telling God he was sorry and that he'd go to Nineveh.

Soon Jonah was on a shore, spit out by the big fish. He went right to Nineveh. There he gave God's message. The people, even the king, changed their bad ways. God forgave them.

And this put Jonah in another bad mood!

The story of Esther
Based on the book of Esther

Why is this person on the Jesse Tree?
- Some sources say that Esther was a descendant of the tribe of Benjamin.
- The story of Esther saving the Jewish people of Persia from death has been instructional for centuries. Her story is meant as an encouragement and inspiration to Jewish people and is part of the celebration of Purim.

Listener's guides
FOR GRADES KINDERGARTEN THROUGH 3
- Mordecai was Esther's _____.
- Why wouldn't Mordecai bow to Haman?
- What did Queen Esther invite the king and Haman to?

FOR GRADES 4 THROUGH 8
- Why did Mordecai advise Esther not to tell others that she was Jewish?
- Why did Haman order others to bow down to him?
- Why did Mordecai refuse?
- What did Mordecai think Esther could do as queen?
- Esther and the other Jewish people _____ and _____ for three days and nights.
- What happened to Esther when she went to speak to the king?

Family and other group discussions
- Discuss times in history when Jewish people were persecuted.
- Compare how laws are made in countries with democracy with how they were made in this story.

Prayer
We thank you, God, for safety. We pray for all those who are not safe today. Amen.

Reflections for the storyteller
The book of Esther is one of only three books in the Old Testament bearing the name of a woman in its title. Its setting is a sumptuous palace in the Persian Empire, between the fifth and fourth century. The book is among the historical stories written in a literary form. It is filled with plots and counterplots, and is skillfully composed. The author lived about 130 B.C., at a time when the Jews had had some successes in throwing off the power of other rulers, but there was always the fear of conquest. Consequently, all Jews needed to be encouraged to fight and even risk death for their people. The story of Esther is just that kind of encouragement. Her bravery, intelligence, and insight still inspire each year in Jewish synagogues when her story is read at the feast of Purim.

The Story

ESTHER WAS A YOUNG JEWISH WOMAN LIVING IN PERSIA when Ahasuerus was king. Wanting a queen of great beauty, he called for the most beautiful women in the country to come to his palace. He chose Esther. Before going to live in the palace, she said good-bye to her cousin Mordecai, who had raised her after her parents died.

Mordecai advised her, "Esther, tell no one that you are Jewish, for there are always those who are against us. Go now, but know that I will not be far away. May God be with you."

King Ahasuerus was a mighty ruler with a large country to govern. He had many workers to keep his kingdom in order. The most powerful was Haman. Now Haman loved this power, and he ordered all people to bow down to him. Everyone did, except one man: Mordecai.

Concerned for Esther, Mordecai now lived near the palace. Haman passed by him each day, and always Mordecai refused to bow. He believed that he should bow before God alone. As a devout Jew, Mordecai chose to risk angering Haman rather than displease God.

Haman did indeed become angry, so angry he wanted to see Mordecai dead. Each day, his anger grew until he wanted to kill not only Mordecai, but all Jews, for they shared Mordecai's religion! He made a plan.

Going to the king, Haman said, "Your majesty, in your country there is a certain group of people living apart, with laws differing from those of every other people. They do not obey the laws of the king. Shall we have them killed?"

Haman did not say who these people were, or how they behaved, and the king did not ask.

"Do with them whatever you please," said the king. Neither he nor Haman realized they had just condemned the queen to die.

Haman arranged that on the thirteenth day of the twelfth month, all the Jews in the entire country of Persia would be killed. A decree declaring this was sent out to all the governors in the kingdom.

Everywhere, Jewish people wept, cried out, and prayed. Mordecai cried loudly and bitterly. But Esther, in the palace, knew none of this. Mordecai sent a message, asking her to convince the king to change the decree.

Esther was filled with fear for her people, but she was also afraid for herself. She sent a message back to Mordecai.

"All the royal servants know that any person who goes to the king without being summoned will be killed unless the king extends his golden scepter. I myself have not been summoned to the king for thirty days. I cannot speak to him."

Mordecai knew that only Esther could save them now, so he sent another message. It said, "Perhaps it was for a time like this that you were chosen to be queen!"

Esther listened to Mordecai's message, her heart heavy, for she knew Mordecai was right. She told the messenger, "Instruct Mordecai to ask all the Jewish people to fast for three days and nights on my behalf. I will, too, and then I will go to the king, despite the law. If I die, I die."

Mordecai and all the Jewish people fasted. They cried out with all their strength, for death was staring them in the face. Esther, too, fasted. She took off her queenly clothing, dressing instead in mourning clothes. She smeared ashes on her face, and her lovely hair became wild. She prayed constantly.

On the third day, Esther washed and dressed in her most enchanting clothes. Feeling small with fear, she walked into the king's court.

The king looked up angrily. Who dared to come in here? Queen Esther staggered from fear and hunger, her lovely face drained of its color. She fell forward, and God changed King Ahasuerus's anger to gentleness.

Anxiously, the king sprang from his throne, taking Esther into his arms. "What is it, Esther? Take courage! You can trust me!" He touched Esther with his scepter, and went on, "Speak to me! Whatever you want, even if it is half my kingdom, it will be granted you!"

She answered, "If you please, your majesty, come today with Haman to a banquet I have prepared. There I will tell you what I request."

The king gladly agreed. That night, he and Haman enjoyed the feast. Again the king turned to Esther, asking her what she requested.

"If it pleases your majesty, I ask that my life be spared, and I beg that you spare the lives of my people. For my people and I are to be delivered to slaughter and extinction."

The king was astonished. "Who and where is the man who has dared to declare this?" he asked.

"It is this wicked man, Haman."

Deeply angered, the king left the room to walk in the palace gardens. Fearing his wrath, Haman stayed with Esther, begging for his life. Desperate, he threw himself at her. The king came back in and thought Haman was trying to hurt the queen. Immediately Haman was arrested—to die as he had wanted Mordecai to die.

King Ahasuerus then decreed that the Jewish people would be safe, and Mordecai would have the job Haman held. Together, Mordecai and Esther worked for the welfare of their people.

SHORTER VERSION

The king chose Esther to become queen because she was beautiful. He didn't know that she was Jewish too.

He didn't know that her cousin, Mordecai, was upsetting Haman, the king's main worker. Haman was a powerful man, and he loved having power. He made everyone bow down to him each time they saw him. But Mordecai refused. He only bowed to God. Haman was getting more and more angry.

But the king did not know any of this.

Haman became so angry at Mordecai that he wanted to kill him. In fact he wanted to kill anyone like Mordecai. Haman came up with an evil plan. "Your Majesty, there is a group of people in your country who do not obey your laws. Shall we have them killed?"

The king agreed. He didn't ask questions.

Mordecai and all the other Jewish people became frightened. Queen Esther was frightened too. They all prayed and fasted for three days. Then the queen gathered up every bit of her courage and went to the king.

He was glad to see her. He didn't know he had agreed that she should die.

Trembling, Esther asked him to spare her life and the lives of her people.

Now the king asked questions and quickly understood. Word went out that no Jewish person was to be killed. But Haman did not fare so well.

The story of Tobias
Based on the book of Tobit

Why are these people on the Jesse Tree?
- The memorable characters in this story have value in showing us the best of Jewish family culture, which would be Jesus' culture. The Archangel Raphael can be seen as symbolically showing us Jesus' priesthood.

Listener's guides
For grades Kindergarten through 3
- Why was the father, Tobit, so unhappy?
- What attacked Tobias in the river?
- Who was Raphael?

For grades 4 through 8
- Name two pieces of advice Tobit gave his son.
- What parts of the fish did Raphael tell Tobias to set aside?
- What reasons did Raphael give to Tobias for marrying Sarah?
- How did Tobit regain his sight?
- Who was Raphael?
- What does Raphael say the others should do each day?

Family and other group discussions
- Do you believe in angels? Have you ever had something happen that could only be explained as miraculous?
- Both Tobit and Raphael's instructions are good advice. Read and discuss if or how you follow them.

Prayer
Creator God of angels and humans, we praise you for the wonders you have given us! Amen.

Reflections for the storyteller
Like the story of Esther, the book of Tobit is considered a historical story written in literary form. Some of the early Greek Bibles include both of these stories in wisdom writings. Today, this story is found in Roman Catholic and Orthodox Bibles.

Tobit and his son, Tobias, are models of wise people. Themes abound, including the importance of observing the laws, doing good works and almsgiving, remaining patient in adversity, respect for parents, and trust in God.

The Story

LONG AGO, A YOUNG MAN NAMED TOBIAS LIVED WITH HIS PARENTS, Tobit and Anna. This is the story of a journey Tobias took for his parents. The journey proved to be mysterious and wonderful.

Tobit had become blind. This left him feeling such great despair that he prayed that he would die soon.

One day, he called Tobias to him, instructing him, "My son, honor your mother. Pray regularly. All your days, keep the Lord's laws. Give to the poor. And marry a Jewish woman. Now I must tell you this: long ago, I deposited a large sum of money with a relative in the town of Media. I want you to go there now to get it back. Find a trustworthy man to travel with you and we will pay him well."

Tobias met a friendly stranger named Raphael. He was a distant relative, he said, and he knew the way to Media. They journeyed together.

As night came on, the travelers stopped to camp by the Tigris River. Tobias went down to the water and waded in to soothe his tired feet. Suddenly he cried out, for a large fish leapt out of the water and attacked him.

Raphael shouted, "Don't let it get away! Take hold of it!"

Despite his fright, Tobias managed to do this and brought the fish to Raphael. When Tobias knelt down to clean the fish, Raphael said, "Set aside the gall and liver for medicines. The rest will make us a fine meal."

The following morning, Tobias asked Raphael about the medicines that could be prepared with the fish. He was surprised by the answer.

"If you burn the liver, the smoke will drive away demons. The gall can be rubbed on eyes that have cataracts, and sight will be restored," Raphael said. "Tonight we'll reach Media, and we'll spend the night with Raguel, who is a relative. Raguel has a daughter, Sarah, his only child. Your father instructed you to marry a Jewish woman. You should marry her."

"I've heard of Sarah," said Tobias. "She has tried to marry seven times, but all of her husbands drop dead right after the wedding! There must be a demon that kills them!"

Raphael shrugged nonchalantly and said, "That's what the fish liver is for. Marry Sarah, and place the fish liver on the fire. The smoke will scare off the demon."

Tobias was not easily convinced, not wanting to become the eighth victim. But Raphael persisted. "Sarah is sensible. She is courageous and beautiful too. Don't be afraid. She was set apart for you before the world existed."

This caused Tobias to reconsider. "Yes, I will marry Sarah," he said, smiling. "Let's begin the rest of our journey."

When the men arrived, Raguel, his wife, Edna, and daughter, Sarah, were delighted to meet Tobias and Raphael. They spoke of Tobit's blindness with sadness. But soon they feasted. Raphael asked Raguel's permission for Tobias to marry Sarah. Raguel and Edna warned of the demon, but like Raphael, they seemed convinced that God would bless this marriage and keep Tobias safe. Raphael retrieved the money they came for, and the wedding was held then.

That night, Tobias built a small fire and placed the fish liver on it. He and Sarah prayed.

There was indeed a demon, but as the smoke rose, it left quickly, escaping to Upper Egypt.

Now it was time for the newlyweds to travel to Tobias' home. Sarah's parents gave them blessings and gifts, and said farewell.

Edna said, "Tobias, before the Lord, I entrust my daughter to your care. Remember, you are now Sarah's love, and she is your beloved. Go in peace."

On the way back, Raphael said to Tobias, "You still have the fish gall. When you see your father, rub it onto his eyes, and he will see again."

When they reached Tobias' home, Raphael and Sarah remained outside, while Tobias went in to greet his parents. Tobit and Anna were overjoyed to have him home again.

"I am home with the money, but I have much more than that," Tobias said. "First, Father, have courage and let me put medicine on your eyes."

Tobit agreed. Soon he was shouting, "I can see! Blessed is God and all God's angels! I can see my son!"

"Then," Tobias announced, "come see your new daughter-in-law!"

Tobit and Anna were joyful. "Welcome, my daughter! Blessed are you and blessed is my son!" Tobit cried excitedly. "Blessed be God's name for all these miracles today!"

Anna embraced Sarah, saying, "Welcome to your new home. Come, let's celebrate!"

Raphael stood quietly nearby as Tobit spoke privately to his son. "We'll give Raphael half of the money you brought back."

Tobias gestured for Raphael to join them. He held out his bag to Raphael, but Raphael put up his hands to refuse. He said, "No, thank you. Do not pay me. Instead, thank God for all that has been done for you. Never stop praising God. Do good, give alms. Prayer and fasting are good, but giving to others and right behavior are even better."

Father and son looked at one another, puzzled.

Raphael went on, "When you saw me eat and drink, you saw a vision. When you prayed to die, Tobit, I was sent to you. For I am Raphael, one of the seven angels who serve the Lord."

Tobit grabbed for his son's arm and both backed away.

Gently, Raphael said, "Do not be afraid. It was God's will that I came to you, so thank God each day. And praise God each day. And now, I must ascend to God." And then Raphael was gone.

So, Tobit, who wanted to die, lived happily many more years. As the angel instructed, he sang God's praises, and gave money to the poor. He and Anna were blessed with seeing seven sons born to Sarah and Tobias. They never saw Raphael again, but perhaps one journey with an angel is enough for a lifetime.

SHORTER VERSION

TOBIT AND ANNA PRAYED EACH DAY and often shared their money with others. But then Tobit became blind. Thinking he would soon die, he called their son, Tobias, to him.

"Tobias, honor your mother. Pray each day. Obey the laws. Give to the poor. And marry a Jewish girl," Tobit instructed. "Years ago I left a large sum of money with a relative. I want you to travel to him and get the money. Find someone you can trust to travel with you. We will pay him well."

Young Tobias soon met a traveler named Raphael. Tobias knew Raphael was trustworthy, but still Tobias had unusual experiences. A fish attacked him as he bathed his feet in a river! Then Raphael knew of a girl he thought Tobias should marry. "Sarah was set apart for you before the world existed," Raphael said. And Raphael was right: Sarah was the one Tobias wanted to marry. But first, he had to show Tobias how to drive an evil demon away from her!

Tobias got married, Raphael got the money, and then Tobias, Sarah, and Raphael traveled to Tobias' home. Another amazing thing happened: Raphael gave Tobias some of the fish and told him to rub it on Tobit's eyes. This caused Tobit to see again!

That was not the last miracle! When Tobit and Tobias tried to pay Raphael, he refused, saying, "Instead of paying me, thank God for all that has been done for you. Never stop praising God. Do good. Share with others."

Raphael went on, "God sent me to you. I am one of the seven angels who serve the Lord." And the angel Raphael was gone.

The story of Daniel
Based on Daniel 5–6

Why is this person on the Jesse Tree?
- Daniel lived much of his life in forced exile, in places where God was unknown. He remained faithful, despite his isolation and threats against him.
- Daniel's story is one of courage, remaining steadfast in adversity, but also of God's love and protection.

Reading this story
Before reading the longer version of the story, explain that from this story comes a famous expression: "seeing the handwriting on the wall." Ask children to listen for this expression and consider what it means.

Listener's guides
FOR GRADES KINDERGARTEN THROUGH 3
- Fill in the blank: Daniel was forced into a place where hungry _____ were kept.
- Circle the right answer: The others who worked for the king felt this way about Daniel.
    - A) They were jealous
    - B) They wanted to be his friend
    - C) They thought he was a good baseball player.

FOR GRADES 4 THROUGH 8
- Where was Daniel's home and where was he forced to live?
- What appeared on the wall during a festival?
- What was the law that King Darius was tricked into signing?
- What did the king say to Daniel just as Daniel was being forced into the lions' den?
- What did King Darius vow to do while Daniel was in the lions' den?
- Name one thing the king said of God when Daniel was unharmed.

Family and other group discussions
- As a young man, Daniel was forced to leave his home and live among people who knew nothing of his culture. Discuss what this must have been like for Daniel at first.
- Describe Daniel's personal qualities.
- Why was King Darius so easily tricked into making such a bad law?
- This story shows God's love and protection through the part about the lions' jaws being sealed by an angel. There are many ways people feel this love and protection. Share stories of your own experiences.

Prayer
Dear God our loving Father, while Daniel was in the lions' den, he may have felt scared, hopeless, and angry. We all have times when we feel this too. Help us to remember, as Daniel did, that we can depend on your continuing love. Amen.

Reflections for the storyteller
Having ravaged Jerusalem, King Nebuchadnezzar of Babylon ordered the best of the Hebrew youth

to be brought to him. Already educated and trained in trades or proven in leadership, they were further educated in the Chaldean language, math, and combat. Daniel was one of these young men. Interested in astrology and astronomy, Daniel interpreted dreams for the king, and he quickly rose to a position of honor. Serving under the next three kings, Daniel remained faithful to his God despite his exile.

The story in the book of Daniel takes place during the Babylonian exile, 590 B.C., but was written between 167 and 164 B.C., when the Jewish people were being persecuted again by Antiochus Epiphanes IV. The purpose of the story was to show Daniel's courage and triumph so that others would maintain faith and hope during their trials.

The Story

THERE WOULD BE NO SLEEP FOR KING DARIUS TONIGHT. He paced back and forth. How could he have let this happen? Because he, Darius, had been tricked, Daniel might be dead now! How could he have made such a mistake? The only hope was that this God of Daniel's would save him. Daniel, the intelligent, wise man who had counseled him all these years, must not die! And yet, how could he not? Darius himself had had him thrown into a pit of hungry lions.

Daniel was a Jew who had been forced years earlier to leave his home in Jerusalem to live in Babylon and serve the king, during Nebuchadnezzar's reign. Daniel had interpreted that king's dreams. When King Belshazzar, the next king, held a great banquet, Daniel's powers were once again made known. During the feasting and singing, a hush suddenly fell over the crowd. For on the wall, just behind the lampstand, a human hand appeared and began writing on the wall! It wrote words that no one could read.

King Belshazzar turned pale and trembled. He promised great rewards to anyone who could tell him what it meant. The queen remembered Daniel's powers, and so he was brought in.

Daniel stood quietly, looking at the handwriting on the wall. "Mene, Mene, Tekel, and Parsin. All three words represent weights," Daniel read. "Oh great king, it means this: 'mene' means God has numbered the days of your kingdom and will bring it to an end; 'tekel' means you have been weighed on the scales and found wanting; 'parsin' means your kingdom will be divided and given to two other kingdoms."

Of course Daniel had been right. King Darius began pacing quicker, remembering that King Belshazzar had been killed that very night of the handwriting, and now he, King Darius, was here because the kingdom had been divided.

After becoming king, Darius could see that Daniel was very skilled and intelligent. Darius had given him much power. Daniel did well in his role, but others, Darius saw now, were jealous. Leaders, called governors, who also had power but not as much as Daniel, tried to dishonor Daniel, but they had not found a way. Until now.

They had come to Darius and said, "Oh King Darius, live forever! We governors have agreed that the king should establish a law, that whoever prays to anyone for thirty days, except to you, oh King, shall be thrown into a den of lions. Now, oh king, sign the document so that it cannot be changed."

The idea pleased the king, and he had signed it. Darius groaned now at the memory. He should have guessed that Daniel was a prayerful man!

Daniel had continued to pray, for as much as Daniel honored the king, he honored God more. Daniel knew of the law, but his love for God was so great, he risked punishment and prayed as usual. And of course, the governors had been watching.

They had come triumphantly to the king and told him of Daniel's prayers. Oh, the anguish Darius had felt! He couldn't let Daniel die! All day, until sunset, Darius had thought and plotted, trying to find a way to save Daniel. But once a law was put into effect, not even the king could undo it. Daniel was thrown into the pit of hungry lions.

Darius's parting words to Daniel were, "Oh Daniel, your God, whom you have served so faithfully, will have to save you."

The king had gone back to the palace, where he vowed he would not eat, but fast until dawn. Sleep would not come.

Finally, the first faint streaks of light touched the eastern sky. Darius was down the steps and out of the palace in minutes. He hastened to the lions' pit. He would call to Daniel. Oh, please, Daniel's God, let there be an answer!

Yet, how could there be?

The king shouted, anguish straining his voice. "Daniel! Servant of the living God! Has your God been able to save you?"

From the depths of the pit came Daniel's voice, "O king, live forever! My God sent his angel who sealed the lions' jaws! I am unhurt, for I am blameless in God's sight, and I have never done you any wrong either, oh king."

Darius was overjoyed and had Daniel released.

Soon after, the king sent out a decree to all his people that said, "May peace be with you! Let all my empire know Daniel's God, for this God saves, sets free, and works signs and wonders in the heavens and on earth. This God has saved Daniel from the power of the lions."

And the faithful Daniel flourished during the reign of King Darius, and on into the reign of the next king.

SHORTER VERSION

Daniel was a wise and smart man. Because of this, four different kings had Daniel work for them. The third king, Darius, especially liked Daniel. However, this king got tricked into putting Daniel into a den of hungry lions! Here is what happened:

Daniel's work was important and he did it so well, King Darius gave him more important work. Other workers became jealous. They wanted Daniel out of the way! They knew that Daniel was Jewish, and that he loved God and prayed every day. They would use that to trick the king.

"King Darius," they said. "We suggest you pass a law that says everyone should pray to you."

The king thought that was a great idea.

"And if they pray to anyone else, have the law say they will be put into a den with hungry lions," they said slyly.

The king was still thinking about people praying to him. "Okay," he said, and made the law.

Of course, a few days later they came to the king. "Daniel prays to his God, not you!" they said.

Oh no! Now Daniel would have to go into the lions' den! Not even the king could change the law!

So good, wise Daniel was pushed into a den with hungry lions.

All night, the unhappy king hoped Daniel's God would save him. In the morning he hurried to the lions' den.

"Daniel?" he called, afraid he would hear only a lion's roar.

"I'm here!" Daniel answered. "My God sent an angel who protected me!"

So Daniel was let out of the den and many people saw that God loved and protected Daniel.

And the king was very relieved.

The Story of Elizabeth and Zechariah

Based on Luke 1:5–14

Why are these people on the Jesse Tree?
- Elizabeth was related to Mary, the mother of Jesus. She was a descendant of Aaron, Moses' brother.
- Elizabeth and Zechariah's son was John the Baptist, the prophet who prepared people for Jesus.

Listener's guides
For grades Kindergarten through 3
- Why was Elizabeth so puzzled when Zechariah first came home?
- What did Zechariah see when he was in the sanctuary?
- Why was Elizabeth so surprised about a baby? How else did she feel?

For grades 4 through 8
- What was unusual about Zechariah when he first came home?
- Why did Zechariah draw rather than write in explaining to Elizabeth?
- Besides having an angel telling her husband, why was Elizabeth so surprised?
- Would Zechariah spend the rest of his life being unable to speak?
- How did they celebrate?

Family and other group discussions
- Zechariah is able to speak after the baby is born and the "Canticle of Zechariah" (Luke 1: 67–79) is wonderful Advent reading.
- The angel who spoke to Zechariah was Gabriel. He also appeared to Daniel. Encourage listeners to guess who Gabriel visits next.
- Help children understand the importance of John the Baptist.

Prayer
Thank you, God, for angels, holy people, and surprises! Like Elizabeth and Zechariah, we await the arrival of a very special child. The time is coming! Amen.

Reflections for the storyteller
All of the previous stories introduce people who lived long before Jesus, who show God's saving work in the history of Israel. However, it is John the Baptist who is specifically referred to as the one who went before Jesus, making the way for his public life. But he is not Jesus' ancestor and did not precede him by years. John was Jesus' cousin, born within months of Jesus. When the angel Gabriel told John's father, Zechariah, of John's eventual birth, Gabriel compared John to the prophet Elijah: even before birth, John was filled with the Holy Spirit (it is here that the Holy Spirit is first mentioned in Scripture). And in true prophetic spirit, the unborn John leapt within

Elizabeth's womb when Mary, carrying the unborn Jesus, approached them.

Like many before them, Elizabeth and Zechariah waited for many years to be blessed with a child. They may even have given up hope. When the news came that they were to have a son, it was so surprising, it rendered Zechariah speechless.

The Story

ELIZABETH LOOKED UP, STARTLED AT ZECHARIAH'S NOISY ENTRANCE. He was usually a calm, orderly man. But there he stood, hair disheveled, hands trembling. His eyes had an almost glazed look. "What is it? What happened?" she asked, hurrying to his side.

Zechariah shook his head. He opened his mouth and then closed it again. Holding his hands out in an open gesture, he looked up as if in prayer. He seemed both frustrated and excited.

"What is it? Zechariah, don't keep me in suspense!" Elizabeth pleaded. She took hold of both of his hands and gazed steadily into his eyes. She had never seen her husband so agitated, and she and Zechariah had been together for a long time. "What is it, dear?" she asked again, trying to keep her voice level. "Has something happened at the temple?"

He nodded.

"Can you tell me?"

He shook his head, pointing to his throat and shaking his head again.

"Does your throat hurt? Did you eat something that has harmed you? Oh, has someone tried to hurt you?"

This time he shook his head vigorously. Then, calmer, he put both of his weathered hands on her cheeks. She could only look at him quizzically. He smiled upon her with love, stroked her cheek, and pointed to her abdomen. She backed away and looked down at her body, then back at Zechariah.

"I don't understand. Why don't you speak? You have never been at a loss for words!"

Zechariah gave a noiseless laugh.

This alarmed Elizabeth greatly. "What is wrong with your voice?" she demanded. He was frustrated now and looked around. Frowning, he turned and reached for the writing tablet.

"You really cannot talk," Elizabeth breathed, bringing her clasped hands to her mouth.

Zechariah sat down and began to draw. Elizabeth stood at his shoulder. As she watched, her eyes widened and she trembled. On the tablet he had drawn an angel.

"You saw an angel, Zechariah?" Her voice was a whisper.

He nodded quickly.

"Were you alone?"

Another nod. He made a simple drawing of a temple and an incense burner.

"You were alone in the sanctuary. It was your time to burn incense?"

Another nod. Then he drew a baby and pointed to her.

Elizabeth frowned. "How I wish I could read!" she lamented.

Zechariah tapped the drawing of the angel, then the baby, and then tapped Elizabeth's abdomen.

"Oh, I want to understand!" Elizabeth wailed.

Zechariah repeated his tapping.

"Angel…baby…me," Elizabeth said.

Then she gasped.

"Baby...me? An angel told you I will have a baby?" She spoke as if the words were fragile.

Zechariah leaped up, nodding, and threw his arms around her. They twirled together, two people too old to have a baby.

When they stopped, Elizabeth gasped a bit and exclaimed, "A baby! We've waited so long. We've prayed so hard. The humiliation we have suffered! But a baby, me, Zechariah?"

He laughed his soundless laugh and pointed to himself.

"Oh yes, you and I, Zechariah, at our age, at long last, a baby!" She clasped her hands and fell silent, in a prayer of gratitude. Zechariah stood with her. Then she turned to him. "Did the angel say if the baby is a boy or a girl?"

Zechariah nodded.

"Boy?" Another nod. "A boy," she said, savoring the sound. "A child, oh, Zechariah, we are truly blessed! He must be a very special child, that an angel of God came to tell you about him!"

Zechariah nodded vigorously.

"We must name him Zechariah." He shook his head. "Why not? Do you want to use your father's name?"

His answer was a strong shaking of his head, and he pointed to the angel on the tablet. For a moment, Elizabeth puzzled. Then slowly she said, "The angel gave you a name too?" A smile and a nod. "What is it?"

Zechariah looked anguished. He could not tell her and Elizabeth could not read. "You know, but you have no way of telling me?"

He smiled sadly. She sighed. Then she looked up at him. "And why can't you talk?" He shrugged, and tapped the angel drawing.

"Something with the angel," she mused. Then alarm rose in her voice. "Zechariah, will you always be speechless? Will our child have a silent father?"

He smiled and shook his head. She smiled back, relieved.

"Well, this certainly is the most astounding day. A baby! A son! And you've been visited by an angel! And you, silent for a time! Why you are, I don't know," she pondered. "Oh, Zechariah, the Lord has looked upon us this day! Imagine, me, an old woman, to carry life!"

He looked at her, his eyes full of love. Then they laughed, and he threw his arms around her. They laughed and cried and laughed again.

SHORTER VERSION

Elizabeth's husband, Zechariah, who was priest, was at the temple. She didn't know that an angel was about to come and speak to Zechariah, with news that her life was about to change for a wonderful reason.

Zechariah was alone when the angel Gabriel appeared to him. How frightened Zechariah was! The angel said, "Don't be afraid, because your prayer has been answered. You and Elizabeth will have a son, whom you will name John. He will be filled with the Holy Spirit even before he is born. He will be great in God's eyes. John will be like the prophet Elijah."

"Both Elizabeth and I are too old to have children!" Zechariah said.

"I am Gabriel and I stand before God. I have been sent to tell you this, but you have not believed me. All this will happen, but until then, you will not be able to speak."

When the angel left, Zechariah joined the other people who were praying. He could not talk at all! Zechariah thought of Elizabeth. How happy she would be with this news!

But how was he ever going to tell her?

The Story of Mary
Based on Luke 1:26-38

Why is this person on the Jesse Tree?
- Mary is the mother of Jesus.

Listener's guides
FOR GRADES KINDERGARTEN THROUGH 3
- What was Mary grinding on the millstone?
- What was Joseph's work?
- What do the angel and Mary talk about?

FOR GRADES 4 THROUGH 8
- How old was Mary in this story?
- Name three things Mary knows about Joseph.
- Which archangel appeared to Mary?
- What are two things Gabriel predicts about Jesus?
- Mary felt _____ and _____.
- Why do you think Mary decided to go see Elizabeth?

Family Discussions
- Can you have courage and still feel fearful?
- Gabriel gives Mary God's message as if he is telling her what will happen. Yet, Gabriel waits for her answer, and Mary clearly understands to give one. What do you think about this in terms of your own experience of God's plans for you?
- Imagine you are Mary. What would you ask the angel? What other questions might you wonder or worry about later?

Prayer based on Luke 1:46–47
My soul proclaims the greatness of the Lord; my spirit rejoices in God.

Reflections for the storyteller
Christ's closest ancestor was his mother. A very young woman when she began that extraordinary relationship, she is one of our greatest models of accepting God's plan for our lives. Much has been written about Mary through legend and traditions, as well as in Scripture. This story looks at the moment when she states her commitment to God's will, when she says yes to becoming the mother of the child Jesus. A few centuries later, she would also be called the Mother of God.

The Story

MARY SCATTERED CORN ONTO THE MILLSTONE. She began grinding, her hands quick and skilled. She would make lentils too, for her meal with her parents. Mary did much of the food preparations now that she was thirteen, for soon she would be making meals in her own house, the home Joseph was readying for her.

Mary thought of Joseph, that good man so carefully chosen to marry her. He was a carpenter, a woodcarver. They would not be wealthy, but Joseph made an honest living.

More importantly, he was a kind and gentle man. And he was very prayerful. Together they would lead a life of God's calling.

The light from the open doorway was suddenly blocked. Mary looked up, expecting to see her mother entering. Instead, there stood an angel!

In a rich, full voice, the angel, who was Gabriel, greeted her. "Rejoice, so highly favored one! The Lord is with you!"

Mary stood up, her legs shaking. She could feel her heart pounding. What did this greeting mean? Gabriel went on, "Mary, do not be afraid."

This angel knows my name, Mary thought. And I'm not sure if I can stop being fearful!

"You have won God's favor," Gabriel said. "Listen! You are to conceive and have a son, and you must name him Jesus, for it means 'God saves.' He will be great and will be called Son of the Most High. The Lord God will give him the throne of his ancestor David. He will rule over the House of Jacob forever, and his reign will have no end."

Mary was stunned. It was too much to understand all at once! She must ask a question, if she could find her voice.

She ventured, "How can this all come about? I am not married yet."

"The Holy Spirit will come to you," the angel explained. "So this child will be holy. He will be called the Son of God."

Mary leaned against the table, trying to take it all in.

Gabriel added, "Your cousin Elizabeth, in her old age, has also conceived a son, for nothing is impossible with God."

Mary looked at the angel, and the angel looked at Mary.

"I am the servant of the Lord," Mary accepted. "Let all you say happen."

With that, Gabriel was gone.

The house seemed very empty without the presence of the angel. Mary pondered what she had just heard.

A baby? A son, who was to be great. He would reign forever? She didn't understand. What would Joseph say? Would he understand? Would he raise this child with her?

What would the next months bring? What would the next years be like? She didn't know, but she had said yes to it. She had said yes to God.

And what was this about Elizabeth? She too was to have a baby? At her age? She and Zechariah must be thrilled. That child to come must be holy too, for the angel had spoken of him. She thought of the angel's words, all of them. Her heart pounded again.

"I will go see Elizabeth," Mary decided. "Elizabeth will understand."

The story of Joseph
Based on Matthew 1:18–25

Why is this person on the Jesse Tree?
- Along with Mary, Joseph was the protector and nurturer of the child Jesus.

Reading this story
Most of this story takes place within Joseph's thoughts. To emphasize the importance of the angel's words, you can choose another person to stand and read the angel's lines.

Listener's guides
FOR GRADES KINDERGARTEN THROUGH 3
- What was Joseph's work? Name one tool he had.
- Who came to talk to Joseph? When did Joseph see this vision?
- What did Joseph decide he would teach Jesus as he grew up?

FOR GRADES 4 THROUGH 8
- How long were Mary and Joseph engaged before they were married?
- Often it is said that Joseph was a very good man because, before the angel spoke to him, he had decided to quietly end the engagement. He would not publicly _____ Mary.
- When the angel first calls to Joseph, he says, "Joseph, son of _____." Who is the angel referring to?
- What is the meaning of the name "Jesus"?
- What is the other name the angel says Jesus will be called?

Family and other group discussions
- God had an important job for Joseph. What was it?
- Do you think God has work for us too?
- Name three people who are doing work that God called them to do.
- Why do you think an angel came to Joseph to tell him of the baby instead of Mary telling him?
- Can we recall other Jesse Tree people who were visited by angels?

Prayer
Dear God, our Creator, show us how to listen for your messages as Joseph did. Please give us courage to do what you ask of us. And thank you for Saint Joseph, whose love and concern helped Jesus grow up to become our Savior. Amen.

Reflections for the storyteller
Joseph, the husband of Mary, was the protector, guide, and nurturer of the child Jesus, along with Mary. In Scripture, he appears only in Jesus' early life, leading biblical scholars to believe he died before Jesus began his public life. His presence in Jesus' early life was very significant, however. So important was Joseph that he was guided by an angel when critical decisions about the child were to be made. This story tells of his first angelic encounter.

The Story

IN THE FLAT-ROOFED, MUD AND STRAW HOUSE BELONGING TO THE WOODCARVER JOSEPH, the sound of sawing and hammering could be heard. Outside, children played and called, mothers cooked, and other trades people in nearby houses were busy at work.

Under Joseph's work-roughened but gentle hands, a table was taking shape. The small room smelled of wood shavings. Joseph's saw, adz, and drill lay nearby.

Joseph put down his saw, and rubbed the back of his neck. It was much too early to quit working. He had other projects to finish. But Joseph had no heart for his work today. Everything that had made sense a few days ago had all changed, and he had a difficult decision to make. Besides, what was the point of finishing the table? It was supposed to be for Mary.

Joseph had agreed, less than a year ago, to marry a young woman. Mary's parents had made the betrothal with him. It was made public. Everyone knew that a wedding would take place a year after the agreement. It had been a happy time for Joseph as he prepared a home for Mary. She was young, but she was intelligent, gentle, and prayerful. Joseph knew they would build a life together based on God's love.

He ached as he thought of her now.

Mary was with child. And the child was not his. How could this be? Mary would not have betrayed him and gone to another man. And yet the fact remained: she carried a child now. Hurt as he was, Joseph would not publicly embarrass her. Of course he could not marry her, but he could break his ties with her quietly.

What else could he do? He would go tomorrow to their home and end the commitment. With a sigh, Joseph went back to work, choosing a different project. Perhaps if he worked hard, he would be able to sleep tonight. He did fall asleep after a light supper. He turned over once, twice. And he began to dream. There, in his dream, stood a magnificent angel. The angel spoke.

Angel: "Joseph, son of David!"

The sleeping Joseph sat up in his dream. He did not want to meet an angel lying down.

Angel: "Do not be afraid to take Mary home as your wife. The child within her has been conceived by the Holy Spirit."

Joseph stared at the angel. First an angel, and now this news!

Angel: "She will give birth to a son and you must name him Jesus, because he is the one who is to save his people from their sins. He will also be called Emmanuel, which means 'God-With-Us.'"

Then the angel was gone, and Joseph woke up. He sat up and looked around, bewildered. The dream came back to him slowly. "Do not be afraid to take Mary home." Relief spread through Joseph like a healing spring over dry stones. He wanted to shout, to dance, to go to Mary right now!

"The child within her has been conceived by the Holy Spirit." Those words came back to him. The relief he felt changed to awe and then to fear. An angel had come to him! What kind of holy woman was Mary for this to happen? What kind of life would they lead? What kind of child would this be, with such beginnings? The angel had said, "He is the one who is to save his people from their sins." Who was this child, with such a calling ahead of him?

Joseph lay back down, exhausted. Of course he would marry Mary. Of course he would care for the child. He would provide for and protect them. The angel said the baby would be a boy. He would teach him his woodworking trade. And together, he and Mary would love this special child.

Joseph lay very still, listening to the night sounds for a long time.

SHORTER VERSION

JOSEPH THE CARPENTER LAY DOWN ON HIS BED. He was sad and confused. That day he had found out that Mary, the young woman he was going to marry, was going to have a baby. Joseph knew he was not the baby's father.

Finally, he fell asleep. In a dream, a magnificent angel came to him. "Joseph, son of David! Don't worry about marrying Mary. Her baby is God's baby. God wants you to help Mary take care of this very special child! Name him Jesus."

Then Joseph woke up. He remembered his dream. This baby must be a very special child! He and Mary would work together to protect, teach, and love little Jesus.

The story of Jesus
Based on Luke 2:1-20

Why is this person on the Jesse Tree?
- Jesus is the reason for Advent and Jesse Trees!

Listener's guides
For grades Kindergarten through 3
- What is your favorite part of this story?
- Why was Jesus born in a stable?
- Who were his first visitors?

For grades 4 through 8
- Why did Mary and Joseph have to leave home?
- Who is Joseph referring to when he says they are of the family of David?
- Describe the journey to Bethlehem.
- What were the streets like in Bethlehem?
- Who helped deliver the baby?
- What were some of the things Mary wondered about after the shepherds came?

Family and other group discussions
- Discuss the physical circumstances. Babies weren't born in hospitals, but at home; where would Jesus be born if Mary and Joseph weren't home? How did not having cars, airplanes, or emergency vehicles affect this birth? Bethlehem was not a large city, so there were probably not many places to accommodate travelers.
- Choose instead not to talk, but to sing Christmas carols.

Prayer based on Luke 2:10-14

Leader: *Do not be afraid. For behold, I proclaim to you good news of great joy that will be for all the people. For today in the city of David a savior has been born for you who is Messiah and Lord. And this will be a sign for you: you will find an infant wrapped in swaddling clothes and lying in a manger. And suddenly there was a multitude of the heavenly host with the angel, praising God and saying:*

All: *Glory to God in the highest and on earth peace to those on whom his favor rests. Amen!*

Reflections for the storyteller
Four thousand years of waiting for the Messiah had come to an end. Abraham and Sarah's faithfulness, Rachel and Leah's sacrifices, Joseph's dreams, David's reign, Isaiah's prophecies, Jonah's trials, Esther's courage—all led to the moment in Bethlehem when the Christ Child would be born. And for the readers of these stories, all of Advent, the time of waiting, has passed. It is now the miraculous night when the darkness is over, for "a child is born for us, a son is given us."

The Story

"IS IT TRUE, JOSEPH?" MARY ASKED, THE JUG OF WATER STILL SLOSHING. She had just come in from drawing water at the well. Joseph was drilling a piece of wood. "Must we travel to Bethlehem?"

Joseph put his tool down and sighed, "Yes, I'm afraid so. I just heard too. Every fourteen years the emperor wants a census taken so no one person can go untaxed. As we are of the family of David, we must go to Bethlehem to be registered."

Mary sighed and sat down. Her young body was heavy with the child to come.

"I'm sorry, Mary; with the baby due so soon, it will be very hard for you. He will probably be born there. I'll do the best I can to make you comfortable," the gentle Joseph promised. "But I am very sorry it happened like this."

"Well, maybe this is part of God's plan, too," she answered, and started preparing their meal.

They began their journey early the next morning. Mary packed food and cloths to wrap the baby in. Joseph readied the donkey with other supplies. When she had what they needed, Mary went to the door and turned to look at the home she and Joseph had made together. When they returned, she would have a son to bring into the house. She closed the door and joined Joseph.

The donkey was a good, dependable little animal, but just getting up onto him was difficult for Mary. Joseph helped settle his wife, then squeezed her hand and smiled at her. Despite her discomfort, she smiled back.

For three days they traveled. Mary rode the donkey while Joseph walked, leading it. They crossed the boggy Plain of Esdraelon and the Judaean plateau. All around them were other travelers, and they joined together, talking. Often they laughed, often they complained. Everyone's life had been disrupted for the census that would only bring them taxes. Mary knew Joseph was glad for the company, for traveling could be dangerous. Thieves roamed the hills, as did dangerous animals. Jackals and hyenas were not uncommon.

Mary appreciated the sympathetic looks and smiles from the other women who saw that her baby would come soon. They understood her difficulties, knew she wished that she was home. Still, she would be glad when they got to Bethlehem, where she and Joseph could find a room and be alone.

Bethlehem was on a hill, and the little donkey struggled up it heroically. Mary felt each step, for she now had begun her labor. She knew this was just the beginning, but within hours, she would want to be lying down.

The town was crowded, much more crowded than the roads they had taken this far. Travelers from all over, as well as cattle, camels, mules, and donkeys, filled the streets. The noise was deafening. Mary rubbed her abdomen and closed her eyes for a moment. She did not see the worried look on Joseph's face.

She remained on the donkey as Joseph made his way through the crowd to the door of the inn. He knocked, spoke briefly to the innkeeper, then returned to Mary.

"They have no more room. They are completely full. The innkeeper said they are bedding down people in the courtyard—" Joseph began explaining.

A labor pain overcame her like a wave and Mary gasped, closing her eyes.

Alarmed, Joseph, said, "It is closer than I thought!"

"This is the first pain like this," she said.

"I must think," Joseph said anxiously. "Don't fall off the donkey! I will be right back!"

He hurried into the crowd, again speaking to the innkeeper. Mary saw the man point to the back of the inn, and Joseph thanked him.

"I've got a place. It's with animals, but there are no people. It will be private," Joseph said when he returned. He began leading the donkey as swiftly as he could through the crowds.

Another pain overcame Mary and she did not answer.

This place was just a simple stable in which a patient ox chewed hay, but both Mary and Joseph were glad to see it. Quickly Joseph scooped up clean hay and spread their blanket upon this. Then he helped Mary down from the donkey and to the bed he had prepared. He led the tired donkey to the corner, and hurried back to Mary.

"Oh, Joseph," Mary said, the difficulties of the past three days welling up in her.

He stroked her cheek. "We're alone now. It's the best we can do. I'm here for you."

Another pain came.

Hours passed this way. Joseph was encouraging, calm, and strong. Mary accepted pain after pain. And then, when the time was right, the baby was born. The miracle happened: God became human.

"He is breathing, Mary, he looks healthy—it is a boy," Joseph said, adding, "Of course."

He held the baby close to Mary so she could see him in the darkness.

"He's beautiful!" she said, reaching for him. "Little Jesus, just as the angel promised. Oh, Joseph, he's beautiful!"

In the darkness, Mary could feel Joseph's smile.

They washed the baby, and Mary wrapped him in the cloths she had brought. Then the baby closed his eyes.

"We'd better sleep, too," Joseph said.

"I'm afraid one of the animals might step on him," Mary said. "Let's put him in the manger while we sleep."

A few hours later, Joseph awoke to the sight of a torch coming up the hill toward them. Mary sat up too. It seemed to be a group of shepherds.

"Hello?" one of them called softly. "We don't mean to disturb you, but is there a baby here?"

Joseph stood up, asking, "Is there something you want?"

Another shepherd explained, shyly, "We were tending our sheep when…when…well, we had a vision. An angel came and told us that a baby had been born here tonight, a child who would save us! The angel said the baby would be lying in a manger, so we thought here might be…" he trailed off, embarrassed.

"Many more angels came then too, singing God's praises," the first shepherd said. "It was so glorious, we thought…"

Mary said, "Come in! Here is the Child, and he is in the manger."

The men, humble, rough shepherds, crowded in. They seemed filled with the awe of the angels, which both Mary and Joseph understood. When the shepherds saw the sleeping Jesus, they were silent and prayerful. Then, each one began praising and glorifying God. As they went back down the hill, Joseph stood in the doorway, watching them go and wondering what would happen next.

Mary picked up the now waking baby. She held him close and stroked his small back. So there had been more angels—angels that came to strangers and announced that her baby would save them! What did this mean? She treasured all these things and pondered them in her heart.

SHORTER VERSION

It was a long trip. Mary sat on the donkey, and Joseph walked alongside her for three days. The baby would be born soon, when they were in Bethlehem. They walked with others, for it was not good to travel alone. On and on the brave donkey walked, and as they reached the town, they struggled uphill to reach it.

Everywhere there were travelers! The streets of Bethlehem were crowded. There were more travelers than there were places to stay. Joseph finally found a place for them, away from people. But it was not away from animals, for it was a stable.

There, Baby Jesus was born. Into a poor stable with animals, the Son of God took his first breath.

Usually when a baby is born, there are people who celebrate. For Jesus, there were people, animals, and angels! An angel came and told nearby shepherds, and while they were feeling surprised and puzzled, the sky was filled with singing angels, all celebrating this new Baby! And the shepherds headed over to the stable, where they welcomed Jesus to this world, and thanked God for the gift of His Son. And Mary held her baby, and wondered about life with little Jesus.

Symbol ideas

The stories may suggest different symbols to different listeners, and participants are encouraged to use creativity and imagination in making the symbols.

Here are just a few possibilities that could be adapted to the activities described in "Methods and Materials":

CREATION: moon over water, earth

ADAM AND EVE: fruit, tree, snake

NOAH: ark, rainbow

ABRAHAM: stars

SARAH: tent, bread

JACOB: ladder of angels

RACHEL AND LEAH: three hearts, entwined

JOSEPH: twelve brothers, coat

MOSES: baby in a basket, tablets of Ten Commandments

RUTH: wheat or barley sheaves

SAMUEL: temple

DAVID: harp

SOLOMON: crown

ELIJAH: raven, chariot

ISAIAH: tongs of fire and coal

NEHEMIAH: wall

JONAH: fish, ship

ESTHER: jewels

TOBIAS: angel, fish

DANIEL: lion

ZECHARIAH AND ELIZABETH: incense burner, angel

MARY: a figure on a donkey, or traditional symbols for her such as a rose or a ship

JOSEPH: hammer, saw

JESUS: star, stable, manger

Creation

Adam and Eve

Noah

Abraham

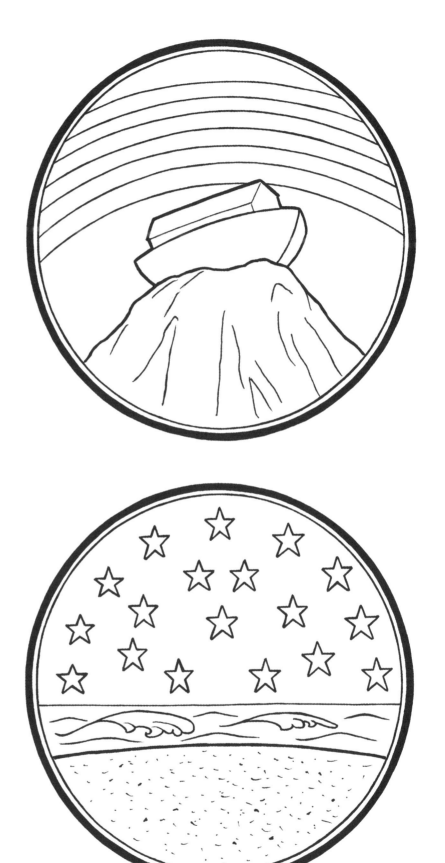

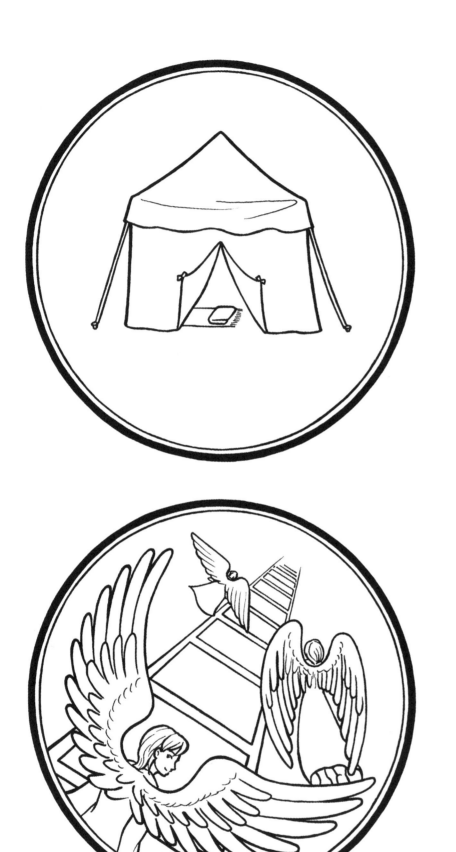

Sarah

Jacob

Rachel and Leah

Joseph

Moses

Ruth

Samuel

David

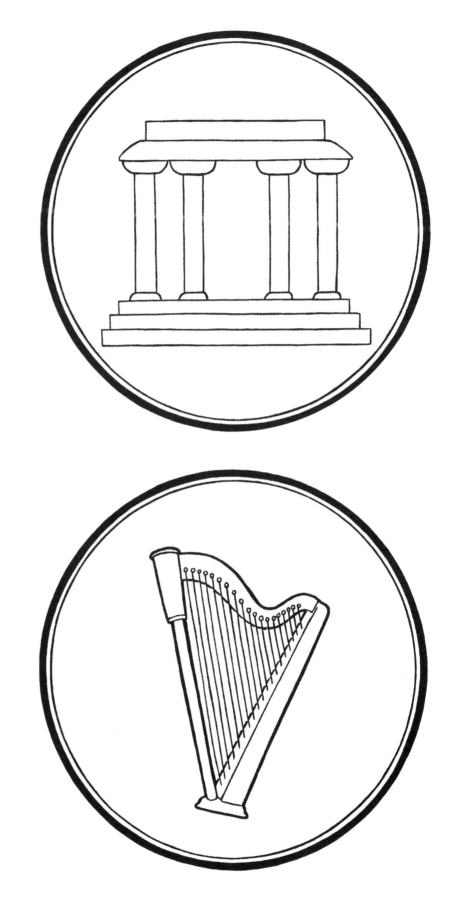

Solomon

Elijah

Isaiah

Nehemiah

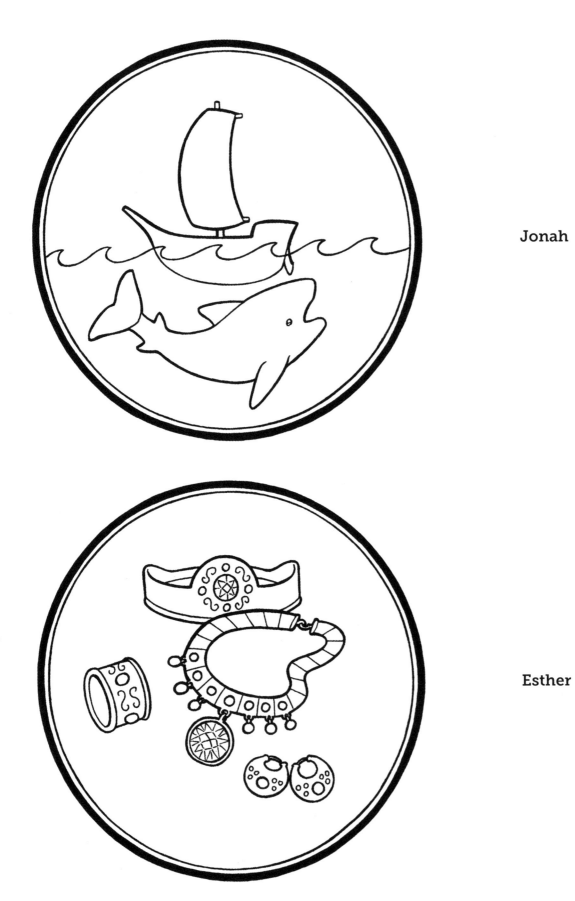

Tobias

Daniel

Elizabeth and Zechariah

Mary

Joseph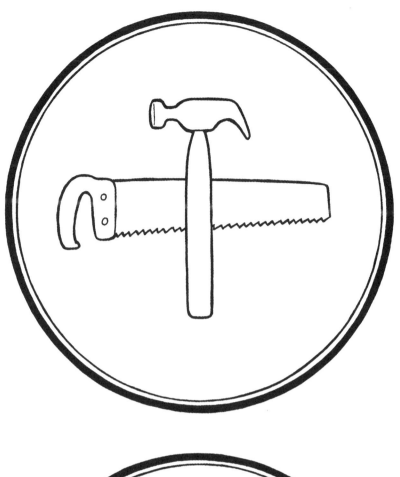

Jesus

ALSO FROM ANNE E. NEUBERGER

All God's Children
42 Short and Joyful Stories for Children
(ages 3 through 8)
These delightful stories give children unique insights into the way other children live in far-off places like India, Turkey, China, Ethiopia, and Iraq. Each introduces wonderful customs and traditions and also offers guidelines for "before reading the story."
104 PP | $14.95 | 978-1-58595-797-2

A Circle of Saints
Stories and Activities for Children ages 4-8
Helps children get to know saints like Nicholas, Lucia, John Bosco, and more than 30 others with these engaging stories told in the framework of the liturgical year.
88 PP | $16.95 | 978-1-58595-750-7

To Walk Humbly
Stories and Activities for Teaching Compassion
and Justice for Ages Ten through Thirteen
Offers 55 wonderful stories from around the world to help young Catholics connect with the social, environmental, and economic problems of children around the globe.
144 PP | $19.95 | 978-1-58595-616-6

To Love Tenderly
Teaching Compassion and Justice through Stories
and Activities for Ages Five through Nine
These compelling stories about children and families from many different countries and cultures introduce children to the realities of poverty, injustice, and abuse of natural resources—and inspire them to make a difference.
96 PP | $14.95 | 978-1-58595-510-7

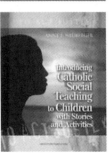

To Act Justly
Introducing Catholic Social Teaching to Children
for Ages Seven through Thirteen
Drawing from the lives of the saints and Christian witnesses, these remarkable stories illustrate the seven social justice principles, the teachings of Vatican II, and the beatitudes in an appealing format.
96 PP | $14.95 | 978-1-58595-222-9

1-800-321-0411
www.23rdpublications.com